CW00551714

Wicca Starter Kit (2 Books in 1) : Wicca for Beginners, Wicca Book of Spells a Guide to Candle, Magic, Herbal, Crystal, Moon, Rituals, Witchcraft and Wiccan Belief

Wicca for Beginners

A Guide to Witchcraft, Rituals, Spells, Moon Magic and Wiccan Beliefs

Karen Spells

Disclaimer

All erudition supplied in this book is specified for educational and academic purposes only. The author is not in any way to be responsible for any outcomes that emerge from using this book. Constructive efforts have been made to render information that is both precise and effective. Still, the author is not to be held answerable for the accuracy or use/misuse of this information.

Foreword

I will like to thank you for taking the very first step of trusting me and deciding to purchase/read this life-transforming book. Thanks for investing your time and resources on this product.

I can assure you of precise outcomes if you will diligently follow the specific blueprint I lay bare in the information handbook you are currently checking out. It has transformed lives, and I firmly believe it will equally change your own life too.

All the information I provided in this Do It Yourself piece is easy to absorb and practice.

Table of Contents

INTRODUCTION

This book is geared toward the solitary practitioner who wishes to discover ways to practice Wicca but is not sure of how to start. The book does not support or recommend any particular Wiccan tradition or ideology; instead, it focuses on the beliefs most Wiccans have in common. Reading this book is an excellent way to begin for those curious about Wicca.

Take time to learn the subtle nuances upon which the craft is based. By doing this, you will gain essential understanding, and you require to genuinely make the most of all the art needs to provide. Wicca is more than a once-in-a-week journey to the church; it is a lifestyle.

If you're reading this book, you probably currently understand Witches and Wiccans are real people, living in the contemporary world-- not the mean, green-faced, frightening old hags seen in popular movies and Halloween outfits.

They are not malicious, and they don't attempt to manipulate anybody through sneaky means.

Although lots of Wiccans and Witches might be deceptive about their work and faith, there is absolutely nothing ominous about what they do. These stereotypes arise from misunderstandings about pagan beliefs discovered throughout Europe before the rise of Christianity.

This has prevented lots of people from knowing anything about the luxurious appeal of the customs for those following the spiritual lifestyle. Happily, you will soon know more about the realities, instead of the misconceptions about Wicca.

Interest in Wicca has increased significantly over the years. This is at least in part, thanks to the internet. Just about twenty years back, those people curious about this subject might have had limited access to important information, especially those without an excellent New Age or Occult book shop anywhere in the area. The internet has made it easy for information to get to whoever seeks it. Not every website is of equivalent quality, of course, and people are mostly advised to overlook anything that does not "feel" right for them. This is true for print sources, too.

Wiccan authors can sometimes be argumentative-- as individuals enthusiastic about any religious beliefs can be-- and you might discover that some sources resonate with you more than others.

This book is meant as a quick introduction to the subject, covering one of the most fundamental concerns that people curious about Wicca tend to have.

We will be checking out the faith of Wicca, the history of its modern-day origins, and the fundamental belief systems that its different traditions commonly hold. Then, we will carry on to magic, as we look at Wiccan practices, including the relationship between witchcraft and magic, and covering a few of the necessary tools and methods involved.

CHAPTER ONE

Understanding Wicca

The Meaning of Wicca

Wicca is categorized as a nature-based faith incorporating a wide array of customs, practices, and beliefs influenced by several sources-- Wiccans typically refer to these sources as "the Old Religion."

There are many types of customs under the umbrella of Wicca, generally with overlapping aspects such as pantheism, polytheism, an emphasis on routine, and deep respect for all living things.

Wicca has been mostly referred to as a shamanic religion. "Shamanism" is a term initially used to refer to ancient religious beliefs found in areas of Asia. Still, it has since been used in describing numerous indigenous customs throughout the world whose origins predate recorded history. Shamanism is mostly called the world's first religion, although it would not have appeared like the significant religions these days with their consistent beliefs and constant practices that span continents.

Features of shamanic traditions include an animistic world view, using altered states of consciousness to interact with the spirit world, and using the knowledge found there for healing and the basic well-being of the community. Shamans were the very first "medication individuals" and were revered in their societies. Like shamans, Wiccans look for a connection with the hidden spirits of nature and work with natural representatives such as stones and herbs for protection and healing.

Wicca is also thought about to be a Pagan faith. Like "shamanism," "paganism" is also an umbrella term. It has been specified in the broadest sense as any religion that is not Christianity, Judaism, or Islam. Still, it's more accurate to say that Paganism involves nature-based belief systems that mostly (however not always) include several deities.

The word "pagan" originates from the Latin, where it implies "country individual," and didn't have any religious association. Later, the name took on an unfavorable connotation when Christianity attempted to stamp out the old beliefs and practices of the country occupants in Europe and other places it looked for to control.

As a nature-based collection of practices and beliefs, Wicca is a kind of paganism, but there are lots of other contemporary Pagan traditions besides Wicca. This difference is intended more at modern-day (or "Neopagan") spiritual movements than the general sense of the word as a category of "faith." "The Old Religion" isn't found in a specific text or location or culture, but is a sort of catch-all name for the many hairs of older spiritual and cultural beliefs that notify today's practices.

While it claims spiritual roots in older pagan and shamanic belief systems, Wicca itself is a contemporary religious belief, of relatively recent origins, and the word "Wicca" as an official name for the faith came about several years after its preliminary starting. Considering that there is no consensus on any particular text, practice, or specific belief, there is a great deal of leeway in regards to who may "claim" to be Wiccan. However, many practices overlap among different customs, groups, and people.

Among the elements of Wicca that distinguish it from other more commonly acknowledged religious beliefs is its emphasis on the feminine, as signified by nature, the Earth, the Moon, and feminine divine beings (or goddesses). The masculine is also represented through deity and is primarily associated with the

Sun, but there is none of the patriarchy typically discovered in other Western faiths.

Belief systems and practices identifying as Wiccan can be highly formalized and consist of hierarchical structures within practicing groups, but can also be very personalized and "free-form."

Wicca's modern history is complete of unusual and intriguing characters whose different contributions to the practice are a subject of much research study and argument by today's historians of the movement. Before diving into the critical points of Wicca's origins, let's look at some of the terms often associated with the name "Wicca.".

Historical Facts About Wicca.

To comprehend modern Wicca, its wisdom and practices, what you'll be doing, and why it's crucial to understand where it comes from. There's been no little effort and debate in understanding Wicca's origins and development. All faiths have myths about their starts, but when it comes to Wicca, the reality is more remarkable than the misconception. There are important reasons that Wicca is called the Craft of the Wise.

Roots

The word itself is a great place to start. Wicca arrived in Britain with the Anglo- Saxons in the mid-5th century. Its roots go back some 5,500 years to the most widely spoken language in the world, called Proto-Indo-European. There are also roots to prophecy, or talking to divinity.

How did Wicca get connected to Witch? Simple: the pronunciation of Wicca is witch-a, and in the 16th century, the Modern English spelling ended up being Witch. The origin of both words provides a different picture from the negative stereotype of the evil, Satan-worshipping hag, and reminds us that there were Indigenous traditions in England, and, throughout Europe and the Fertile Crescent (the Middle East), long before the arrival of Christianity and the vicious stereotype.

Wicca and Shamanism

Wicca is rooted in shamanism, humankind's earliest spirituality. Some call it the Old Religion. Today shamanism is still practiced throughout the world by around 370 million Indigenous individuals, despite centuries of harsh colonial domination.

A modern-day form of core shamanism, made up of essential practices common to lots of shamanic traditions but without specific cultural overlays, is being significantly practiced by the modern descendants of immigrants from Europe, Russia, Africa, and in other places who are also uncovering their Indigenous ancestral traditions.

Shamans are masters of balancing, harmonizing, and uniting inner and outer, the visible and invisible, the world, and the spirit. Across the world, shamans use comparable strategies to open themselves to the Sacred and to live in consistency with nature. They shift and begin their awareness with ecstatic practices like drumming, chanting, dancing, journeying, praying, vision-seeking, communion with sacred plants, working with natural energies and aspects, routine and ceremony.

Not everyone ends up being a shaman, but anyone can practice shamanism. Not everybody ends up being a Priest/ess, but anyone can practice Wicca. For hundreds of years, practicing

Wicca, practicing Witchcraft, or even being accused of being a Wiccan could get you eliminated.

Rebirth

In the early 1930s, an impressive group of English critics went looking for the religious beliefs of their ancestors. Why that moment? Perhaps it was a response to100 years of the Industrial Revolution, with its damage to land and people, and the penalizing effects of World War I and the Great Depression.

Inspiration may also have come from the counterculture of Romantics, Spiritualists, Suffragists, Theosophists and the mystical, incredible motion made famous by the Hermetic Order of the Golden Dawn-- a metaphysical society with such distinguished members as Lady Gregory and the poet W.B. Yeats-- all trying to find a different type of divinity that consisted of the Feminine Principle.

These brave souls lived in the middle of enormous stone circles, gigantic mounds and chalk giants sculpted into hillsides stories of fairies and myths of Avalon, the Green Knight and Sir Gawain, seasonal stag-antlered dances and the faces of Green Men carved in churches, Goddesses called Bride, Brigid and Brigantia, from whom some say the name Britain came, and Gods of the forest such as Cernunnos and Herne. There was seasonal rejoicing remembered in regional folk traditions and protected within the Christian calendar, and old Gods and Goddesses very finely disguised as saints. Everything was amber in which proof of an earlier life resided.

There was also the advanced theory of a fantastic Egyptologist and Suffragist, Dr. Margaret Murray, the 'grandmother of Wicca.' Murray's book, The Witch-Cult in Western Europe, released by Oxford University Press in1921, argued that Witchcraft had been a pan-European religious practice with beliefs, rituals, and systems as developed as that of any.

Whatever the inspiration, it's challenging to recover a religion from shattered shards and a bad reputation. Three covens, or groups, appeared in England in Hampshire's New Forest and Norfolk and Cheshire. The covens were discreet and hidden, but in 1951, the Witchcraft Law of 1735 was rescinded, and Witchcraft burst into the general public's awareness in the individual of Gerald Gardner, a retired British civil servant.

Gardner wrote many of the very first books on Witchcraft by a practitioner and spoke publicly and to journalists-- no little accomplishment given the lingering stereotypes. And he dealt with a few of the most crucial females in Wicca, like Doreen Valiente, the coven's High Priestess. Valiente wrote the famous Goddess invocation The Charge of the Goddess, and she and Gardner expanded the rites and practices that formed the structure of the Gardnerian custom.

Gardner declared that he practiced the faith Murray had described, calling it Wicca, and her theory ended up being Wicca's well-accepted 'misconception of origin.' Years later, after thorough scrutiny, practitioners and historians concluded that the Gardnerian custom was not an unbroken, hereditary, pan-European tradition matching Murray's theory.

Today, many people still register for Murray's theory as a literal fact. Always, other Wiccans appreciate her recognition of stereotypical truths that continue to resonate-- a Great Mother Goddess, a Horned God of forest and field, a little community arranged into groups (covens) with skilled Priestesses and Priests, using thrilling practices, the celebration of seasonal, lunar rites and holy days, initiation rites and the keeping of a book of wisdom called the Book of Shadows.

Wicca settled and started to grow beyond the British Isles with the rediscovery of other forgotten Euro-Indigenous traditions and pantheons of divine beings from faiths that existed before the Abrahamic religious beliefs (Judaism, Christianity, and Islam), particularly Goddesses, which were incorporated into Wiccan practice and cosmology. Ladies found a spiritual home that honored them as religious leaders; publishing and the internet also connected people and offered access. Leaders who were unafraid of persecution emerged into the public eye to challenge stereotypes, and the motion grew and generated a more comprehensive revival of Modern and euro-indigenous pagan traditions.

Today, there are lots of variations and varied family trees and customs in Wicca, each with its organizational structure. Many have included religious organizations, churches, or temples, and while the law and academics now recognize Wicca as a spiritual practice, many practitioners choose the term spirituality. In formal studies, the number of followers of Wicca varies from a couple of hundred thousand to several million worldwide.

Wiccans are lawyers, physicians, rock stars, truck motorists, dog fitness instructors, and Unitarian ministers and as most likely to be your neighbor next door as your dental expert. Wiccans are, literally, everywhere.

Wicca's legitimacy does not need to be obtained from its past, but from the profound, transformative spiritual experiences, worths and insights it provides professionals every day. In this sense, Wicca is a brand-new mental motion, and its (re)birth is among the rarest and significant occasions in human history.

The origin of Wicca traces back to a British occultist named Gerald Gardner in the early 1940s. Gardner's frustration with both Ceremonial Magic, the only "occult" option and Christianity, prompted him to create something that appears to be different in some ways.

Gerald Gardner's religious practice was based on pre-existing spiritual principles, which he integrated in a new way to form a brand-new system. His mixing of ceremonial magic with hereditary Witchcraft and Masonic ritual was nothing less than genius. And, with the assistance of individuals like Doreen Valiente, Dion Fortune, Ross Nichols, and other notable scholars, he could develop a vibrant and new religion.

Witchcraft, or Wicca, as we understand it today, is not the sole survivor of antiquity, nor is it a modern creation. Instead, it is a mix of many various spiritual persuasions. Even though Pagan rites, Shamanic customs, and Goddess worship predate Christianity, there is still no reputable proof of a recognized Wiccan religion before the year 1951.

Gerald Gardner broke the vow of secrecy after the final repeal of the English Witchcraft Act in1951, by accepting the New Forest Coven.

Today, many Wiccan organizations in the United States and Europe support Gerald Gardner's ideas.

The Known History

The modern origins of Wicca can be traced back to the British Occult motion in the late 19th century. A couple of crucial figures credited with advancing and establishing Wicca as a faith are Gerald Gardner, Cecil Williamson, Patricia Crowther, and Lois Bourne. Gardner (1884-1964) is widely credited as being the creator of Wicca. However, he and his fellow witches didn't use the term "Wicca" as a recognizing term, but instead called their practice "Witchcraft," (in some cases reduced to "the Craft") or "the Old Religion." Gardner did describe the members of his custom as "The Wicca," but "Wicca" as a name for the religion was not used frequently up until the 1960s as it affected the U.S. and Australia.

Gardner had ended up being interested in a theory advanced in the early 1920s by anthropologist Margaret Murray (1863-1963), which held that a pagan religious belief with a family tree going back to ancient times had existed in secret throughout the rise and supremacy of Christianity in Western Europe. Murray called this faith a "witch cult" and asserted that its professionals were arranged into 13-member groups or covens, and worshipped a male "horned" god.

In the early 1940s, Gardner's exploration of occult and mystical experiences influenced him to develop a brand-new incarnation of the witch-cult, and he formed the Bricket Wood coven. Blending concepts from Murray with other sources such as Freemasonry, ceremonial magic, and the work of other Occult authors, Gardner's custom broadened the divine being praise to include a female goddess component along with the male god.

In 1947, Gardner met and befriended Aleister Crowley (1875-1947), a well-known occultist and writer. They had checked out and taken part in a variety of spiritual and esoteric customs from worldwide, consisting of Buddhism, Jewish mysticism, Hinduism, the Tarot, astrology, and more. Crowley's writings had a considerable impact on Gardner, who included some of the rituals devised by Crowley in his work. It was Crowley who coined the spelling of "magick" with a "k" to distinguish his type of magic from other "ritualistic magic"-- and even stage magic--practices of the time.

Crowley is a complex figure for lots of Wiccans today. Some of the practices he took part in were considered to be scandalous, and his role in the history of the religious beliefs helped perpetuate an incorrect association between Wicca/Witchcraft and Satanism.

It must be remembered that "Satanism" belongs to the Christian world view and not a pagan idea, which Wicca does not, and never did, integrate, endorse, or practice "Satanism" or the worship of anything "evil.".

Crowley had a reputation for being misogynist and racist, which are mindsets incompatible with the Wiccan way of life. At any rate, the custom now referred to as Gardnerian Wicca began to grow as Gardner brought other interested Occultists into his coven, consisting of several women, among whom was Doreen Valiente (1922-1999). Valiente ended up being the High Priestess of Bricket Wood in the early 1950s and revised much of the initial material the coven had been using, in part because she felt it had too much of Crowley's influence. Ultimately, Valiente parted methods with Gardner over what she perceived to be his careless attempts to make modern Witchcraft known to the masses, and his decision to restrict the power of ladies in the coven in response to their criticisms.

Valiente formed her coven in 1957 and went on to study Witchcraft with other leading figures in the movement, eventually composing several prominent books that assisted introduce the evolution of Witchcraft from a secret society phenomenon to a widespread, highly customized practice. Other notable figures in the growth of the Craft were Alex Sanders (1926-1988), who established the Alexandrian tradition of Wicca, and Raymond Buckland, who formed the Seax-Wicca custom in the early 1970s. Born in 1934, Buckland is credited with bringing Gardnerian Wicca to the United States and has written dozens of books on Witchcraft and other esoteric subjects.

It was during the 2nd half of the 20th century that what is jointly called Wicca spread from England to the rest of the United Kingdom and the United States and Australia, branching off into numerous different traditions. While those who follow the Gardnerian customs and its direct offshoots commonly draw a difference between Wicca and other, non-Wiccan witchcraft, many individuals identify as Wiccans no matter the origins of their particular practice. These consist of individuals following Dianic, Celtic, and Georgian customs, in addition to "diverse" methods adapted from a variety of traditions.

The Unknown History

Regardless of the claims of Margaret Murray, Gardner, and others to have discovered and restored an authentic ancient tradition, scholastic historians never might see much undeniable evidence to support the "witch-cult" theory. And within the motion, leaders' claims of hypnotic trance states, being "descendants" of ancient Witch lineages or "reincarnations" of Witches from past centuries, were, in some cases, questioned, even by other Witches.

Stress and anxiety over the viewed degree of validity and credibility of Wicca may have caused some Witches to take strong positions in favor of one tradition over others, one belief over another, and to argue nonstop about it. It's also possible that these concerns of authenticity led some Witches to draw more greatly from what is understood about traditions from other cultures and other mystical practices than from the particular product that was expected to link the contemporary religion straight to its ancient past.

Yet, with all that is unidentified about the past individuals and cultures that Wicca draws motivation from, what is understood is that there was some energetic phenomenon that was magical enough to keep a hold on humanity, even though the rise of Christianity and its eventual domination of the parts of the world most regularly associated with the "ancient religion." European folk magic customs, a lot of which are included in Wiccan magic, were perhaps descended from this very same source. And we likewise understand that pagans and shamans of cultures around the world looked for to engage with the hidden world in comparable ways, through music, dance, and modified states of consciousness.

It may be enough to say that what the initial creators of modern-day Wicca did was develop new kinds through which individuals could tap into the magical, bridging the space in between the modern and ancient worlds with new expressions of a magical energy that has continuously existed. There may be a dizzying range of analyses of these brand-new forms, but there suffice commonness amongst them, and adequate people participating, to make it clear the "Old Religion" is back, and here to stay.

CHAPTER TWO

Forms of Wicca

Gardnerian Wicca

Gerald Gardner set a precedent for the contemporary Wiccan motion. At some point during the late 1930s, Gardner was introduced to a genetic Witch called Old Dorothy Clutterbuck, who started him into a group called the New Forest Coven. Before this, Gardner had been added to the Masons, Oriental mysticism, and the Golden Dawn system of ritualistic magic.

Gardner's new faith did not blossom overnight. It took years to best, with the input of other Witches and occultists.

The religion that Gardner developed, Gardnerian Wicca, worries the praise of the horned God and the Goddess. A High Priestess usually heads covens, and they have three levels of initiation, paralleling those of the Masons. Religious celebrations happen at the eight seasonal shifts, and complete moons are considered to be a time of terrific power and potential.

A lot of Gardnerian groups work skyclad (naked), and polarity (the balance between the manly and feminine) is emphasized. Covens tend to have equivalent numbers of male and female initiates, and couples are motivated to join.

Alexandrian Wicca

Alexandrian Wicca, a spin-off of Gardnerian Wicca, was founded in the early 1960s by Alex Sanders and his better half, Maxine. He proclaimed himself "King of the Witches"; he declared to have been initiated at age Seven by his grandma.

Alexandrian Wiccans use Kabbalah, the excellent system of the ancient Enochian and Hebrews, the established magical language for angels, which has its alphabet and grammar. Covens often meet once a week.

Dianic Wicca

There are two distinct categories of Dianic Wicca. The first category is Old Dianic, formed in the early 1960s by Morgan McFarland and Mark Roberts. This original branch of Dianic Wicca places primary significance upon the Goddess, but still acknowledges and honors the Horned God as her accompaniment.

The 2nd branch of Dianic Witchcraft is feminist in orientation. Only females are permitted, and just the Goddess is worshiped. Frequently covens have lesbian participants just. The majority of groups are loosely structured, routines are often experimental and spontaneous, and meaning will differ from one group to another. The focus is mostly on the female aspect, and there is usually a political list attached to the group.

Diverse Wicca

This branch of Wicca covers individuals and groups who do not follow any single tradition, but who instead incorporate the elements of many different cultures into their practices. They deal with different divine beings from various pantheons, rather than focusing on one specific god and goddess. Diverse Wiccans mix and match events, myths, and symbols according to choice and experience.

Hereditary/Traditional Wicca.

The witchcraft practiced within a family that claims a lineage predating the Gardnerian revival is regarded as traditional or genetic.

Typically, the Hereditary Witch originates from a family that practiced folk magic and organic medication. When it comes to a true Hereditary Witch, there will be proof of the direct line of descent from ancestors who were Witches.

Hereditary/Traditional Witches have a slightly different approach to doing things than the post-Gardnerian Wiccans do. Generally, the majority do not use the basic set of excellent tools, but depend on everyday items to work as symbols of their craft. The importance is put on nature divine beings, fertility, appeals, amulets, and organic potions. Complete moons are usually used for divination, and the working of magic, and seasonal celebrations concentrate on the prosperity and protection of the family.

CHAPTER THREE

WhatDoWiccansBelieve?

Is Wicca a religion?

Wicca is far less organized and noticeable than other faiths such as Judaism, Christianity, or Islam, Wicca has actually been acknowledged as being entitled to the same spiritual defenses by courts in the United States. It is even considered in the chaplain's handbook of the U.S. Army. In the UK, Wiccan priestesses and priests are authorized to function as jail chaplains, but Wicca is not formally acknowledged as a religion.

Wicca is often referred to by those outside the practice as a "cult," possibly because it's called one in the Oxford English Dictionary. This word is also challenging. "Cult" has several neutral significances, though regrettably for Wiccans, it's typically associated with negative images and groups with charismatic leaders like the followers of Jim Jones. Regardless, "cult" is not generally used by Wiccans to describe Wicca.

Many authors on the subject describe Wicca as a religious belief, particularly those who identify as Wiccans. Others who use the terms "Wicca" or "Wiccan" to explain their beliefs and practices do not necessarily regard Wicca as a faith that they follow or "belong to." This may be because Wicca has no central text, prophet, or another source of authority like the dominant Western religions, and its structures and kinds of worship differ exceptionally commonly. It might also be because the word "religion" has associations that some Wiccans are not usually comfortable with.

For numerous reasons, the number of people identifying as Wiccans in predominately English-speaking countries is more difficult to accurately approximate than it is for more dominant religious beliefs. Many people choose not to disclose their religion in a culture where it is not respected and is frequently sufficient, even hostilely opposed. Others who may freely identify as Wiccans are innumerable, as there are no official holy places for them to be members of.

Some scholars evaluating random phone surveys over the past few decades have estimated that close to one million people around the world consider themselves Wiccans, with the majority found in the U.S. and the U.K. Whatever the actual count might be, it's clear that the numbers are increasing progressively in the 21st century, as more knowledge about the religious beliefs become offered and widely shared.

What's the distinction between a witch and a Wiccan?

Depending upon who you ask, there's a significant distinction, or there's not much (if any) difference.

In regards to language, the words "witch" and "Wicca" are somehow related, as "Wicca" was the Old English word that later ended up being "witch." Nevertheless, among Wiccans, the relationship between the two concepts is less black-and-white--some Witches determine as Wiccans.

Witches who don't, and Witches who don't have a preference. Some Wiccans do not determine as Witches.

The different uses of these words can be seen throughout contemporary composing about Wicca and Witchcraft. In addition to the name of the religion, some authors use "Wicca" as a particular word in place of "Witch," but most use "Wicca" as a plural term, implying that some (or all) Wiccans can be jointly called "the Wicca.".

While the words "Wicca" and "Wiccan" tend to be capitalized--specifically about the faith and its members-- however there appear to be no hard and fast guidelines relating to whether to capitalize the words "Witch" and "Witchcraft" or leave them in lower case.

Some fans of Wiccan customs which do not adopt the name "Wicca" as a personal identifier feel no need to recognize with a capital "W" for "Witch" or "Witchcraft." Others think that capitalization of these terms is essential in differentiating Wicca as an official religious beliefs and developing a cultural regard for it. In the spirit of respect for those who feel profoundly about acknowledging Wicca as a religion, this book capitalizes all four terms.

What's the difference between Wicca and Witchcraft?

Wiccans who don't identify as Witches do not use the term "Witchcraft" in association with their practice of Wicca-- they don't use magic, and they distinguish between Wicca as a spiritual practice and specific relationship with the divine, and witchcraft as a practice that is not always spiritual.

Many Wiccans do blend magic into their practice to varying degrees, and might usee "magic" as an interchangeable term with.

" Witchcraft" (frequently reduced to "the Craft") in association with Wicca.

In reality, some Witches who practice Witchcraft do not identify as Wiccan at all.

What does Wicca pertain to magic?

Once again, it depends upon who you ask, and for Wiccans who do not practice magic of any kind, the response is most likely "nothing." Many Wiccans do consist of magic in their practice, to the point that the two are combined in many Wiccan books and resources-- including this particular book!

Many Witches will refer to their practice of magic as Witchcraft, but might use either term. And of course, the word "magic" is also a bit tricky, as it has its own set of meanings.

" Ceremonial magic" is older than Wicca and was an initial impact for what would eventually end up being Wicca. However, it's, in fact, a practice in its own right-- to put it simply, not part of the religious beliefs. This ritualistic magic has numerous differences from the magic practiced by Witches. Ceremonial magic was derived from occult customs through secret societies like the Freemasons and the Hermetic Order of the Golden Dawn, and is typically quite elaborately ritualized. The term "high magic" is, in some cases, used to differentiate it from Witchcraft, which is called "folk magic" or perhaps "low magic" by numerous of its practitioners. Some who practice ceremonial magic may determine as Pagans but are not Wiccans or Witches. Some merely discover as magicians.

What some call "useful magic" is a sort of ceremonial magic focused on attaining common life improvements, such as healing physical or emotional ills, drawing in love, and improving one's financial resources. Some Wiccans see this form of magic as non-spiritual and distinct from Wicca, but others mix the two by performing magic in positioning with their deities and for the good of all, instead of just for their own personal gain.

Wiccans Believe Everything Is Connected

Many people discover Wicca in pieces and bits. Maybe Wiccan routine empowers them. Or the Wiccan respect the rhythms and cycles of nature that pleases them. Or magic interests them. To fully discover and comprehend the significance in Wicca, a person needs to grasp the vast image of the Wiccan worldview.

A couple of core concepts underlie all of Wicca, and if you understand these standard principles about the divine and the entire world, then Wiccan beliefs and practices make sense. This chapter supplies the background to comprehend Wicca as a full-fledged spirituality and a specific method of experiencing and translating the world.

Swimming in a Divine Sea of Energy

You will discover one principle that is essential to the Wiccan belief, which "is: Everything is linked."

Everything that exists becomes part of an unbroken circle of vibrating energy. You might discover it uses to picture truth as a web of energy. Some individuals refer to this idea as the web of life or nature's web. Most Wiccans think that Deity is imminent (is right here, today, and all-present in the world) and also appears in the environment (is apparent and quickly viewed).

The majority believe that whatever exists streams from the Deity. The Divine is regarded as the source of all life. Some Wiccans even think that the entire universes are the living body of Deity.

The belief in Deity gives faith. Nobody can prove that the universes have a Divine source; however, but honestly, there is one big, connected, boundless network.

Finding Kinship right in the Cosmos

The Wiccan perception of an interconnected world isn't merely a magical, spiritual concept. Modern science, particularly cutting-edge ideas in quantum physics, supports the concepts of life's affiliation and interdependence. Below are some of the leading theories that mix thoroughly with Wiccan belief.

Going quantum: Matter versus energy

Individuals see the real world as a bunch of steady and independent objects. However, that's not precisely the reality. Modern science exposes that matter and energy are not different.

Energy streams in waves that form patterns. What you view as a different thing (a pet dog, a bird, or a tree) is just a pocket of truth where the energy is more dense, according to quantum physics

Quantum physics.

Physical matter is made up of particles and atoms, which are comprised of smaller components, referred to as subatomic particles. A subatomic particle is not precisely a little dot of matter that scientists can hold still and analyze; it's better described as a bit of dancing point of energy. These particles can't be comprehended as different units. Scientists can describe subatomic particles just by discussing how they show one another. The best way to meaningfully describe these particles is to discuss the way that they adjoin.

String theory.

A subatomic particle is not pointlike; however, it is made of a small loop. Like an incredibly- thin elastic band, each particle contains a vibrating, dancing string. Like a guitar string, each low string can vibrate. Every line equals; the only distinction is how it vibrates. Each series has various vibration like each guitar string develops distinct musical notes. The motions of the series-- the "note" it produces-- identify the kind of particle it will be. These itty-bitty vibrating strings comprise everything in the universe-- all physical matter and all forces (such as gravity). These strings vibrate throughout space-time.

We reside in space-time. Space-time consists of three dimensions of area (width, depth, and length) and the proportion of the time. All objects and all events exist in these four measurements. Well, that's what scientists utilized to believe. According to the string theory, space-time can have up to nine measurements of space, plus the analysis of time.

Wicca meets string theory.

String theory unites matter and energy and validates the Wiccan view that the universe from the smallest particles to the most significant planetary systems operates by the same principles and is made from the same stuff. At all levels, life is adjoined.

They are spreading out the turmoil.

String theory indicates the interconnection of life at all levels, big and small. Chaos theory deals just with the vast and super-complicated.

Chaos theory

Chaos theory recommends that the weather and other massive, complicated systems in nature have an underlying order, but they are virtually unforeseeable and chaotic. The issue with predicting the weather and the habits of other big systems is that life is very conscious of altering conditions. Minimal modifications can have significant impacts. Any small inaccuracy in assessing the preliminary conditions results in growing errors in the calculations.

The significant lesson here is that any action, no matter how little or irrelevant, can impact everything else. Earth's ecology is a network of relationships. All the members of the Earth's environment are synergistic. The success of the entire community depends upon each living thing, while the success of each living thing depends significantly on the success of the city. This concept forms the core of Wiccan principles.

Looking at Gaia

The world is made up of specific parts, and these parts may function by themselves. The pieces are all made of the same energy and are connected to form one giant whole. For instance:

- An individual cell forms part of a person.
- Human beings belong to life on Earth.
- Earth belongs to the planetary system.

The Gaia hypothesis

Climatic chemist James Lovelock, microbiologist Lynn Margulis, and others have established a theory referred to as the Gaia hypothesis, in honor of the Greek Goddess of the Earth. This principle explains all of Planet Earth as a living system that organizes itself and keeps all its parts in balance.

Lovelock and Margulis never suggested that Earth is a sentient being (a mindful, imaginative being). However, others have expanded the theory to reach this concept.

Enfolding and unfolding

Physicist David Bohm propounded a theory of physics on the concept that truth unfolds from one original, boundless source. Numerous charge card has these pictures. Each little piece of a hologram can recreate the entire image. In other words, each part includes all the information about the full. This structure is standard in nature. A small seed contains all the info to grow a tall sunflower.

The Holographic Universe

Based upon this design, Bohm (a former coworker of Einstein) suggested that the details for the whole universe are held in each of its parts. For Bohm, the explicate order is the different parts of the world that we see. The link order enfolds all these parts into one whole. All beings, including people, are born from this source, are connected, and share consciousness.

Wicca meets the holographic universe

The relatively new design of the Holographic Universe reflects a worldview that Pagans have held given that the most ancient times: We are all part of the Divine energy; we are all linked, and our fate is inexorably linked. Nature flows from Deity, and Wiccan spirituality focuses on the event of our connection with nature and the human place in the web of life. Much of Wiccan practice is dedicated to developing a relationship with the Divine energy, in which we are permanently ingrained.

Wiccans Believe In Deity

Most, although not all, Wiccans believe in a creative being or force. However, how Wiccans perceive and experience the Divine is unique to each person. Wiccans stretch the concept of Deity to the extreme.

Two individuals may conveniently call themselves Wiccan. They might carry out the same rituals, work the same magic, and happily practice side by side, but they might have drastically various principles of who, or what, Deity is. The majority of Wiccans would instead celebrate their distinctions than become religious beliefs in which everybody must conform to the same idea or look for the same experience.

The following areas outline some manner ins which Wiccans define the Divine. It's an overall appearance in some typical manner ins which individuals think about Deity. The details may assist you to comprehend the variety of Wicca. You might not be able to pigeonhole your own experience according to these explanations. Do not attempt to intellectually choose one of these classifications and then expect your spiritual life to conform to one of these examples outrightly. Let your religious life show what is right for you, whether it shows one, a mix, or none of

the following examples.

- **Honoring The One**

Lots of Wiccans believe in a Deity who is the source of the cosmos. The Wiccan names for this Divine power consist of, but not limited to: The All, the Ultimate Sacred, The One, the Great Mystery, Creative or Supreme Being, the Source, the All-Encompassing Unity and the Life Force.

Many think that this Deity is too vast, too complicated, too incomprehensible, and also limitless (can something be too infinite?) for the human mind ever to comprehend. Although most Wiccans acknowledge this concept of Deity, they have lots of ways of defining, perceiving, or otherwise making the principle of the Divine more workable.

- **Deity as life force**

The Divine being is the ultimate support of all that exists. All of reality is a whole network of vibrating energy, which energy is the Goddess. The entire universes is the body of the Goddess (including physical and psychological strength).

The Goddess is immanent, indicating that She is right here, today and is all-present in the world.

Deity as the Supreme Goddess.

Deity is regarded as the supreme Goddess. She is considered to be the source of all life, and the vital force flows or unfolds from Her. Goddess is the only or the main Deity, and She is a supernatural, imaginative being. He is the child, consort, or symptom of the Great Goddess if there is a God. She is understood primarily in the Mother element, often called Earth Mother or Great Goddess. She also is transcendent, in the sense that She is a thinking and creative being independent of the cosmos.

This theory is in keeping with the ideas of some early Paganism.

- **Deity as the Source**

The outlook is not standard, and some Wiccans are reconciling their spiritual beliefs with the mentors of the new physics. Lots of scientists and philosophers have recommended this kind of idea. Still, scientists and paleontologist Pierre Teilhard de Chardin and physicist David Bohm are mainly accountable for the real popularity of this particular Deity theory.

This holy intelligence existed before the universes were formed, and all reality comes from it. Because all of the truth flows from the Source, everything is linked. The Source encompasses all time and space, all dimensions, and all planes of presence. All things that exist emerge from the Source, and then everything enfolds back into the Source, in a constant cycle.

Individuals continually have brand-new experiences, and they acquire knowledge and insight. All this new info becomes part of the Source Energy, and the Source expands and develops. Individuals are part of the Source, so they likewise progress and grow, reaching higher levels of awareness. People become part of that evolution and even play an essential function in advancement.

Our intelligence and insight permits us to view the Source. Our consciousness acts as the bridge between this holy intelligence and the natural world.

Through our consciousness, we take in detail from our experiences in the world and share that information with the Source; and through our awareness, we also can receive information from the Source for usage on the planet. In computer terminology, this is a feedback loop of info.

This view follows contemporary physics. The language is present; the theory isn't so different from the old Pagan idea of the primal Goddess as both life force and innovative being.

- **Honoring the Two**

Numerous Wiccans think in The One, also referred to as the ultimate Source of the cosmos, but they see it as a type of energy field having two poles. The God and the Goddess are opposite poles of the Divine, and Wiccans honor or praise both the female and male aspects of Deity. Most of the Wiccans probably hold this view or a variation of it. However, no one can state for sure.

CHAPTER FOUR

A World In Balance: Polarity And Duality

In Wicca, particularly in particular customs, polarity or duality is an essential principle. Many Wiccans honor the duality or polarity in nature and have included the idea into their spirituality.

Here's the concept: Energy flows in two opposite directions in nature. Numerous Wiccans see the Divine in the very same method; the Goddess and the God resemble two poles on the same battery. If they were genuinely separate beings, according to these Wiccans, confusion and mayhem would rule in the world.

The Goddess

The Goddess is the womanly aspect of the Divine. She is understood as the Great Goddess, Earth Mother (or Mother Earth), the Universal Mother, the Great Mother, the Lady, and lots of other names. Numerous cultures throughout time have worshipped her.

Maiden, Mother, and Crone

In lots of traditions of Wicca, the Goddess is carefully associated with the Moon. She typically is deemed having three aspects that correspond with the phases of the Moon:

The Maiden (the Waxing Moon) represents independence and youth. She is the virgin Goddess. She is typically related to a female's wild nature and is shown as a forest Goddess in the business of animals.

The Mother (the Full Moon) represents offering birth (not only to kids, but to concepts, insight, and jobs), and likewise nurturing, sensuality, sexuality, and creativity.

The Crone (the Waning Moon) represents age, maturity, knowledge, and the command for respect.

Throughout the eight main Wiccan holidays, the Goddess shifts in Her aspects from Maiden to Mother to Crone and back to Maiden. She provides birth to the Divine God kid, nurtures Him to the adult years, joins with Him and ends up being pregnant, and rebirths Him to start the seasons again and turn the wheel of the year.

The importance of the Goddess for ladies

Since it provides a powerful spiritual alternative to ladies, lots of scientists assume that the factor that Wicca is overgrowing is. Unlike most faiths, within a Wiccan circle, a woman can honor and worship the feminine Divine.

The significance of that truth can't be overestimated. In the doctrines of lots of religions, females are, at the finest, thought about inferior to men and subject to their control. At worst, women are considered as the source of sin in the world. This religious conditioning exceptionally harms the minds of ladies.

Within Wicca, women are equal; they are not "the other." Women have authority and autonomy equivalent to males. Their lives can be changed when females experience their holiness and when they have the chance to direct their spirituality.

The God

In a lot of Wiccan books and groups, God is given less page count or time than the Goddess. In American culture, the majority of people are familiar and even conditioned to see Deity as male. The Divine womanly is a harder concept for lots of people to get their minds around, so I dedicate more of this chapter to discussing the idea.

God is regarded as the male aspect of the Divine. He frequently is represented as the Sun and is sometimes related to forests and wild animals. Many cultures, throughout time, have worshipped him. In a lot of customs of Wicca, the God is considered equivalent to the Goddess. The bulk of Wiccan groups, traditions, and covens, think about males and females to be equal.

Honoring the Many

Many Wiccans honor or praise several Deities. These may be different aspects or parts of the one Divine Source, or they may be separate entities. They may be nature spirits, supernatural beings, or something else. They may or may not have human qualities. You might hear them called The Old Ones, The Mighty Ones, or The Ancient Ones.

Some Wiccans honor and praise the Goddess and the God and feel no pressure to pick a called Deity or Deities. Other Wiccans feel very highly that individuals need to select one or more called Goddesses or Gods to honor, worship, or communicate with.

All the Gods form part of The One

Many Wiccans recognize Deity as The One-- the infinite, unknowable Source of the universes. They believe that Deity is enormous and too intricate for people to comprehend, so these Wiccans may choose to define minimal aspects, types, or parts of Deity as Goddesses and gods. Simply put, the many Goddesses and Gods are various elements or components of one Great Source. Wiccans get to that Source by interacting with their Deities. Or, possibly, that one all-encompassing Source selects to take lots of different kinds to be understandable and perceivable to people.

The Gods are separate beings

The Goddesses and Gods are different, unique, and called Divinities. Numerous different Gods and Goddesses exist, and each has its personality and realm. A few of these beings may be Gods (male) or Goddesses (female), and some might consist of both sexes or be able to move sex and gender.

Honoring the Self

For some Wiccans, Deity might be the Higher Self, Deep Self, or Soul Self (an individual's spiritual essence),

Symbols, Archetypes And Realities

For some Wiccans, Deity lies just within the human mind and imagination. Deity might be a reality or insight occurring from the personal unconscious mind or the collective unconscious shared by all humans.

The unconscious mind has two parts:

The individual unconscious is the place of everything that isn't presently mindful; however, it can be, consisting of memories that you can call quickly and those that you have buried deep in your mind.

The collective unconscious holds the built up understanding and experiences of all humankind. It carries impulses, which are patterns of behavior. An inspiration tells a bird to construct a nest, and a turtle to go to water. Humans likewise have intuitive ways of acting.

The unconscious mind doesn't have the language to express these human habits and experiences. It communicates only in photos. It uses symbols. A sign is an image or item that represents something else. The cumulative unconscious uses archetypes, symbols that prevail to all humans. A model is not an image, however a tendency for human beings to represent specific concepts with a particular sign.

An individual may be an agnostic or an atheist and still practice Wicca. Wicca is a massive camping tent. Each person's understanding and experience of Deity is unique.

Also, some Christian groups today think that anybody who worships a God aside from theirs is following Satan. It's real that Wiccans don't worship the Christian God, nor do people of numerous other religions all over the world.

Wicca and Satanism were and are entirely various and different systems of beliefs, ethics, and practices.

Believing in Magic: Where Science Meets the Craft

Magic is a process of moving and directing energy to achieve a goal, so any description of magic needs to begin with some talk about power. That's what this chapter uses: a neat little description of the different sources and types of energy.

This chapter demystifies magic. Here, you can learn what magic is. It's effective. It's profoundly stunning. And it's a genuine force that numerous Wiccans use to enhance their lives and to assist others. Furthermore, magic is a method to deepen the relationship and honor with Deity and to help the Earth and her occupants.

Tapping into Different Kinds of Energy

Lots of various cultural customs divide the self into three parts. Each part represents a different kind of human energy and power. This department is accessible in modern psychology, in numerous types of Shamanism (particularly. the Hawaiian Huna tradition), in the mentors of Jewish Kabbalah, and lots of cultures of Wicca and Witchcraft (specifically in the Faery or Feri tradition).

In this chapter, I use the model of the Three Selves-- the Spirit self, the conscious mind, and the unconscious mind-- to plainly define the three types of energy and power that are important to Wiccans, especially in the working of magic.

Drawing from the Divine: Energy of the Spirit.

The energy of the Spirit-Self is called the Aumakua in Hawaiian Huna Shamanism and the Neshemah in Kabbalah. Different books on the Craft describe this energy as Deep Self (in Starhawk's novels), High Self, Divine Self,

Real Self, or Bird Spirit. Modern psychology does not have a comparable concept; however, the Spirit-Self is directly connected to the unconscious mind.

The Spirit Self is a person's innermost resource, the place that transcends discomfort and limitation. This is the part of the Self that shelters an individual's essence, the true nature. It transcends time, existing before birth and after death.

I was thinking and talking: Energy of the mindful mind.

The energy of the mindful mind is referred to as the ego in contemporary psychology, the Uhane in Hawaiian Huna Shamanism, and the Ruach in Kabbalah. In various books on the Craft, you may see it called Talking Self (in Starhawk's books), Middle Self, or Talker.

The conscious mind is the part of the brain that functions on a daily level. The mindful mind experiences the world and interacts with language (numbers and words). It is the reasonable mind that organizes and analyzes. It likewise makes ethical judgments and manages social relationships. It translates and discovers meaning for the unconscious mind's feelings, emotions, and images. The mindful mind makes it possible for a person to comprehend spiritual practice on a logical level. Nevertheless, the unconscious mind is essential, too, to link the mindful account with the Spirit-Self or Divine Self.

Going Deep: Energy Of The Unconscious Mind.

Did you understand that the human embryo briefly establishes structures that look like the gills of a fish, along with a visible tail? This short stage of social advancement drastically reflects our animal ancestry and our long evolutionary journey. In addition to the body, the mind, too, consists of an exceptional residue of the ancient past: the cumulative unconscious, a part of the unconscious mind.

The energy of the unconscious mind is called the id in modern psychology, the Unihipili in Hawaiian Huna Shamanism, and the Nephesh in Kabbalah. In different books on the Craft, you may see it called Younger Self (in Starhawk's books), Low Self, Child Self, Young Self, Child Within, Inner Child, Animal Spirit, or Fetch.

The unconscious mind has two parts: the individual unconscious and the cumulative unconscious.

- The personal unconscious.

The personal unconscious is the location of individual information that is beyond present awareness or awareness, including memories that an individual can call up quickly, and those buried deep within the mind.

- The collective unconscious.

The collective unconscious is the inherited part of the brain. It holds the accumulated understanding and experiences of all humanity (and perhaps animals). The collective unconscious mind doesn't have lots of language abilities. It experiences the world and expresses itself in images, emotions, experiences, and dreams. It uses signs. A sign is an image or item that represents something else.

The collective unconscious contains our impulses, which are patterns of habits. Instinct tells a bird to develop a nest, and a turtle to go to water. People likewise have intuitive ways of behaving. Impulses are ways of acting. The cumulative unconscious also consists of archetypes, which are methods of perceiving. A pattern is a propensity for human beings to represent specific ideas with a particular symbol. These stereotypical symbols appear in religious beliefs, dreams, myths, and fairytales throughout all human history. The Earth Mother is an excellent example of an archetype, and the Hero is another prime example.

What does all this mind-stuff have to do with Wicca? Whatever! Many of the practices of Wiccan routine-- mainly routine performed for the function of working magic are shown to trigger the unconscious mind.

Specifically, the working of magic is more productive, more efficient, and more satisfying when the unconscious mind is included. The unconscious mind is mighty, and the images, signs, emotions, and other information hidden within it are a valuable resource for bringing and comprehending the self about modification.

Wiccans use primal images, smells, textures, and sounds to arouse the unconscious mind. Candle flames, incense, stones, and drumming are some examples of traditional components of the Craft that are utilized for this function. Spells are made to rhyme to engage the unconscious in the magic. Wiccans often raise power, which means to induce a light hypnotic trance state, to activate the unconscious mind for magical work.

Engaging the unconscious mind is essential in the working of magic for the following reasons: Exciting the unconscious mind makes a person open up to experiencing Deity since the Spirit Self or Divine Self communicates straight with the unconscious mind.

The unconscious mind drives specific habits, as well as feelings. The conscious mind may rationally understand that certain practices are unsafe or disadvantageous (for example, smoking cigarettes, drinking, or extreme gaming). However, modifying habits might be strict unless the unconscious is aroused and encouraged to play a function in personal change. Magic engages the unconscious mind, and after that, the unconscious mind influences the individual to make the magic work. This is the power of the idea.

The unconscious mind can assist create the power to shape and direct energy to change the Self or alter the world. The cumulative unconscious also may offer a link to the signed up with the awareness of all human beings, to the species as a whole. Subtly shifting the energy in the collective unconscious may produce modification on the planet beyond the self.

In addition to Deity, some Wiccans might welcome the presence or help of other kinds of energy forms or beings. These might consist of:.

Forefathers: A real relative or someone else who has passed on. Some Wiccans contact ancestors for recommendations or assistance, or to deal with exceptional psychological problems. Whether and when an individual contacts ancestors depend on the person's outlook on the afterlife, reincarnation is a frequently held belief in Wicca. However, if a soul has reincarnated, the ancestor might not be offered for counsel.

CHAPTER FIVE

The Wheel of the Year

The Wiccan year is not the same as the standard Gregorian calendar, which begins on January 1st. Instead, it follows the four seasons, marking the development in the Earth's path around the Sun (which appears, of course, to be the Sun's journey around the Earth) and the corresponding changes to life in the world. Wicca has eight significant holidays, or Sabbats, 4 of which are "solar holidays": Summer Solstices and the Winter, and the Spring and Autumn Equinoxes. The other four Sabbats, or the "Earth celebrations," take place near the "cross-quarter days" in between the solar vacations, and are based on older pagan folk festivals which are believed to have been connected to the life process of animals and farming.

Keep in mind: The dates for the solar Sabbats are offered as a range to account for distinctions in the Sun's position in the sky relative to where one lives. The seasonal names for the Solstices and Equinoxes, as well as the seasonal associations with each Sabbat, are likewise different in the Southern Hemisphere.

The existence of 8 Sabbats, rather than four, acknowledges that the contemporary delineations we mark between "the four seasons" are somewhat artificial. For instance, Spring does not all of a sudden become Summer on June 21st; it has been relocating that instructions for a long time before the modern calendar acknowledges it as "Summer.".

An old name for the Summer Solstice is actually "Midsummer," acknowledging that Summer has been well underway by the time the Sun reaches its zenith in the sky. The cross-quarter Sabbats mark the "seasons in-between seasons" and assist the ongoing transitions along the Wheel of the Year. The Sabbats are thought about "days of power" and are marked by Wiccans, Witches, and other Pagans of lots of customs.

- **Winter Solstice (Yule): December 20-23**

Considered in most Wiccan customs to be the beginning of the year, the Winter Solstice is a celebration of the rebirth of the God. It is the shortest day of the year, providing a welcome pointer that even though the cold season is still only getting underway, it doesn't last forever, as the days will begin to extend once again after this point. Some consider the first Full Moon after the Solstice to be the most powerful of the year. This is a joyful holiday commemorating light, in addition to preparation for a time of peaceful, inner focus as the Earth rests from her labor.

Amongst many Wiccans, the vacation is more frequently called "Yule," a name obtained from midwinter celebrations commemorated by Germanic people. "Yule" is still referenced in modern Christmas carols, and much of the traditions surrounding the Christian vacation, such as wreaths, Christmas trees, and caroling, have their roots in these older traditions. It was common for the Christian churches to "adopt" pagan vacations, repurposing them for commemorating saints or essential occasions, as a way of drawing individuals away from the Old Religion.

- **Imbolc: February 2**

Imbolc marks the first stirrings of Spring, as the long months of Winter are almost previous. The Goddess is beginning her healing after the birth of the God, and the extending days signify the conditioning of the God's power. Seeds start to germinate, daffodils appear, and hibernating animals begin to emerge from their slumber. It is a time for ritual cleansing after a long duration of inactivity. Covens may perform initiation rites at this time of new beginnings.

The name "Imbolc" is stemmed from an Old Irish word utilized to describe the pregnancy of ewes and has been, in some cases, translated as implying "ewe's milk" in referral to the birth of the very first lambs of the season. It is also called "Candlemas," and sometimes "Brigid's Day" in Irish customs. Linked with beginnings of development, it's considered a festival of the Maiden.

- **Spring Equinox (Ostara): March 20-23**

At the Spring Equinox, dark and light are lastly equal again, and development accelerates as both the light from the still-young God of the Sun and the fertility of the Earth grow more powerful. Gardening begins in earnest, and trees send blossoms to participate with the pollinating bees. The equal length of day and night produces time for balancing and bringing opposing forces into consistency.

The name "Ostara" comes from the Saxon Eostre, the Goddess of Spring and renewal. This is where the name Easter originates from, as this is another holiday that was "combined" with the Christian tradition.

- **Beltane: May 1**

As Spring begins to move into Summer, the Goddess begins making her transition into the Mother aspect, and God matures into his full effectiveness. Beltane is a fire celebration, and an event of recreation, love, and sex. It's at this time that the Goddess couples with God to ensure his renewal after his death at the end of the life process. Fertility is at its height, and the Earth prepares to thrive with new life.

The name "Beltane" comes from an ancient celebration commemorated throughout the Celtic Isles that marked the beginning of Summer, and is derived from an old Celtic word meaning "bright fire." The ancient Irish would light considerable fires to purify and protect their livestock, and jumping over fires was thought about a way to increase fertility and luck in the coming season.

- **Summer Solstice/ Midsummer: June 20-23**

Long thought about one of the most magical periods of the year, the Summer Solstice regards the Goddess and the God at the peak of their powers. The Sun is at its highest level, and the days are at their longest. This is a celebration of the abundance of sunshine and heat, and the physical symptom of wealth as the year heads toward the first of the harvests. It's a time of ease and short rest after the work of planting and before the work of harvesting begins. Some customs call this Sabbat "Litha," a name traced back to an old Anglo-Saxon word for this time of year.

- **Lammas: August 1**

Lammas signifies the beginning of the harvest season. The very first crops are generated from the fields, the trees and plants start dropping their fruits and seeds, and the days are growing shorter as the God's power begins to subside. This is a time for providing thanks for the abundance of the growing season as it begins to wind down.

The word Lammas comes from an old Anglo-Saxon word pairing meaning "loaf mass," and it was traditional to bless fresh loaves of bread as a method of celebrating the harvest. Lammas is at the same time called "Lughnasa," after the famous festivals in Ireland and Scotland held at this time to honor the Celtic god Lugh, who was connected with the Sun.

- **Fall Equinox (Mabon): September 20-23**

The harvest season is still in focus at the Autumn Equinox. The animals born during the year have grown, and the trees are starting to lose their leaves. Preparations are produced in the coming winter season. The God is making his exit from the real airplane and heading toward his mythical death at Samhain, and his supreme renewal at Yule. Then again, the nights and days are of equal length, signifying the short-term nature of all life, no season lasts permanently, and neither light nor dark ever overpowers the other for long. As with the Spring Equinox on the opposite side of the Wheel, balance is a style at this time.

The Autumn Equinox is thought about in some traditions to be "the Second Harvest," with Lammas as the first and Samhain as the last of 3 harvests. A more current name for the holiday is "Mabon," after a Welsh mythological figure whose origins are linked to a magnificent "mother and child" pair, echoing the dual nature of the relationship between the Goddess and the God.

- **Samhain: October 31**

Thought about by many Wiccans to be the most crucial of the Sabbats, Samhain is the time when the part death plays in the cycle of life is acknowledged and honored. The word "Samhain" originates from old Irish and is believed by numerous to mean "Summer's end." However, others trace it to a root word significance "assembly," which may describe the joint event of a pagan festival, particularly during the harvest season. As the Sun aspect, God retreats into the shadows as night starts to control the day. As the God of the Hunt, he is a pointer of the sacrifice of life that keeps us alive through the long winter season. The harvest is complete, and the sacred nature of food is appreciated. Amongst some traditions, this is viewed as the "Third Harvest."

Other and Wiccan pagan traditions view Samhain as a point in the Wheel when the "veil" in between the spiritual and material worlds is at its thinnest, and the days around Samhain are considered exceptionally reliable for divination activities of all kinds. Forbears are honored and interacted with at this time. A number of the Halloween traditions still celebrated in contemporary cultures today can be traced back through the centuries to this festival. Pagans of the old times left food offerings for their forefathers, which became the modern-day custom of trick-or-treating. Jack-o-lanterns developed from the practice of leaving candle-lit hollowed-out root veggies to direct spirits checking out in the world.

Some Wiccans in the Celtic customs think about Samhain, rather than Yule, to be the beginning of the year, as the death and rebirth aspects of production are seen to be inherently joined together-- death opens the space for new life to take root. Honoring the ancient Celtic view of the year having a "light half" and a "dark half," their Wheel of the Year starts once again on this day, the first day of the dark half of the year.

- **The Esbats**

In addition to the Sabbats, the Wiccan year consists of 12 (sometimes 13) Full Moon celebrations, known as the Esbats. While the Sabbats tend to focus event on the God and his association with the Sun, the Esbats honor the Goddess in her association with the Moon. Covens traditionally satisfy on the Esbats to celebrate a particular element of the Goddess, such as Aphrodite, in the event of abundance, or Persephone, in a routine for renewal. They work with the Goddess to bring about recovery and assistance for their communities and members, and frequently work for the good of the full world.

The Full Moon is also seen within the context of the Wheel of the Year, with names and seasonal attributions for each. For Wiccans dealing with specific elements of the Goddess, the particular goddess called upon during an Esbat will frequently correspond with the time of year. For example, Aphrodite is an appropriate goddess to celebrate abundance under a Summer Moon. In contrast, Persephone, with her underworld associations, is better suited to work with under a late Autumn or early Winter Moon.

The names for each Moon might vary from custom to custom; however, they are usually related to the time of year and the corresponding level of abundance and activity of life in the world, along with the Sun's point in its journey around the Earth. In the Northern Hemisphere, the most common names for the Full Moons in Wiccan routines are as follows:

Month	Moon Name
January	Cold Moon (also Hunger)
February	Quickening Moon (also Snow)
March	Storm Moon (also Sap)
April	Wind Moon (also Pink)
May	Flower Moon (also Milk)
June	Sun Moon (also Strong Sun and Rose)
July	Blessing Moon (also Thunder)
August	Corn Moon (also Grain)
September	Harvest Moon
October	Blood Moon
November	Mourning Moon (also Frost)
December	Long Nights Moon

Many Witches think about astrological influences in addition to seasonal influences and will work according to the specific sign the Moon is in while complete. They will describe the Moon appropriately, such as the "Gemini Moon" or the "Aquarius Moon."

If more than one Full Moon occurs in a given calendar month, it's called a Blue Moon. Happening roughly when every two and a half years, this is thought about an especially busy time in lots of Wiccan traditions, and individual attention is paid to working with the rare energy of a Blue Moon.

CHAPTER SIX

The Role Of Responsibility, Ethics, And Personal Connection With Deity

Wicca is more of a spiritual path. It is mostly concerned with the experience of the Divine and personal discovery. Wicca has no holy book or any written teaching that has been given through the ages for all Wiccans to follow. Wiccans develop their sacred texts of practices, lessons, spiritual experiences, and their understanding. Wicca doesn't have a hierarchy of leaders who counsel people on how to live and praise or those who ensure compliance with religious laws. Each Wiccan maintains a relationship with Deity, and each Wiccan acts as clergy.

Wiccans do have concepts and ethics that direct their behavior, and their objective is to stabilize personal freedom with obligation and regard for life's sacredness.

Building a Personal Relationship with the Divine

To self-directed people, Wicca is a wondrous and liberating venture. For people who want direction and structure in their spiritual lives, Wicca is not a great personal choice. This section checks out Wicca's absence of hierarchy and dogma and the encouragement of its strength, self-determination, individualism, and self-reliance.

Sending dogma to the doghouse

Individuals of many religions believe that Deity, usually referred to as God, is transcendent. Because people can't trust their natures, religious rules inform individuals what to do. Spiritual dogma defines the laws, mentors, beliefs, and concepts of religious beliefs, along with the consequences of breaking the laws. The laws and rules, like God, rise, separate from the world. They are infallible and undeniable. People should follow the laws and regulations, despite the personal expense.

Religious dogma and authority eliminate a person of the obligation of choosing on his or her actions. People abide by the spiritual power because they believe that the institution understands more, is more powerful, and is less likely to be corrupted than the person. They admit that the leaders in the institution can be relied on to know God's will.

Wiccans don't see themselves as different from a Deity. Their Goddess and/orGod is both transcendent and immanent. That implies that Deity is all present on the planet. People originate from and belong to the Divine energy, and the Deity is within everybody. Divine being is a supernatural innovative idea and action; but also remains connected to that creation. Wiccans think that they have a direct relationship with Divinity. They interact with the Goddess and the God themselves, and they do not require dogma or spiritual authorities to manage their frame of mind or direct their will or habits.

Wicca varies from many of the mainstream religions because it does not have a central authority with different levels of clergy who make or propound rules for all of Wicca. Whether the government acknowledges, the Wiccan clergy differs by the regional laws and whether the clergyperson seeks out such acknowledgment. Recognized clergy hold no unique location as part of some centralized religious body that supervises the Craft. Instead, Wicca is comprised of loosely linked and independent, little groups that specify their own spiritual beliefs and practices.

A lot of these little, independent groups do have leadership. The leaders supply assistance and instructions, but they generally don't exercise control over members. Wiccans separately choose how to think and practice.

Many small groups (called covens) have High Priests and Priestesses, or leaders with some different titles, who render their skills to the group and control its activities. Many Wiccan groups have levels of initiation; people advance as they grow and study in the Craft. Some of the groups have a Council of Elders who provide ongoing wisdom gotten during their long experience in the Craft. Nevertheless, in Wicca, leaders do not have control over others.

If a leader has proven experience, offers essential suggestions, and provides needed abilities, the group respects him or her and cooperates voluntarily. Still, nobody in Wicca is obligated to follow the leader.

Every Wiccan is seen as a Priest or Priestess. Each is considered to be clergy because they have direct access to Deity. Wiccans are expected to control or direct their own spiritual lives.

Doing the Right Thing: Ethics and Obligation

One of the most significant charges against the Craft is that it has no morality. Wiccans often are viewed as immature "if it feels great, do it" types who decline to follow the customs of good and decent folk. That's simply not true. Wiccans have a strong sense of ethics, and a brief trip to most Wiccan Websites shows that Wiccans spend a lot of time quibbling about the subtleties of principles and specific duty. Wiccans care a lot about what is wrong, and why. They generally are great people, but the basis for their policies is different from most traditional faiths.

Lots of Westerners see Deity as transcendent, as over and above the world. Human beings are separate from God, and they are independent of each other. People turn to spiritual dogma and organizations to help them live and analyze God's will.

Wiccan belief is quite different. The following concepts are significant to Wiccan practice:

People are connected in an interdependent circle or web of life. Because people are linked to each other, rather than separate, a Wiccan understands that doing damage to others eventually triggers damage to himself or herself.

Those concepts are the basis for the Wiccan Rede and the Threefold Law, which are the heart of Wiccan principles.

Following the Wiccan Rede

The eight words of the Wiccan Rede are; "And it harm none, do what ye will."

These words are the primary ethic of Wicca, referred to as the Wiccan Rede. The name rede indicates counselor recommendations. Some Wiccans think that the Wiccan Rede has been passed down through history. Some believe that it stemmed from Gerald Gardner.

Despite its origins, most Wiccans try to follow the Wiccan Rede, sometimes called simply "the Rede," and consider it to be the helping principle for their lives.

Following the Rede implies carrying out your own will, but acting in ways that trigger the least damage to yourself, others, the Earth, and all humans.

Wiccans generally analyze the Rede to mean that a Wiccan must "live and let others live, while appreciating the sacredness of all life. They need to think seriously about the effects of their actions before they act. Many Wiccans have broadened the scope of the Rede. They feel that apathy, disregard, and failure to work, to stop violence, abuse, suffering, or injustice, also breaches the Rede in some way.

Wiccans have the belief that life as a whole embodies Deity; Deity is all-present on the planet. To trigger damage to anything or anybody is to act contrary to the demands of the God and Goddess.

Following the Rede makes it a little complicated, though. It advises Wiccans not to cause harm to anyone. What about scenarios when a Wiccan is in the form of danger? Are Wiccans permitted to safeguard and protect themselves, even if they need to harm an enemy? Can a Wiccan protect or secure a family or neighborhood? Should a Wiccan damage one individual to save another person? What about cases when a severe injustice is causing lots of people to be harmed? Should a Wiccan action in and assist, possibly causing harm to a single person or group for the higher good of the community? Or should the Wiccan refuse to damage anyone and let wickedness go unchecked? Do Wiccans violate the Rede if they consume (and, therefore, harm) animals? Ask these questions at a Wiccan event and view the mix of emotions.

Wicca isn't simple—people practicing the craft deliberate seriously on these crucial questions.

They are accepting the consequences: The Threefold Law.

You might be familiar with the science of turmoil theory and the butterfly result. The concept behind the method is that all of life is a complicated system. A little change at one place in the network can lead to a significant impact somewhere else.

Everything that exists is connected, and any action, no matter how small or insignificant impacts everything else.

Negative or harmful energy not just hurts the target of the power, but the negativity and damage remain in nature's web and affect all of life, including the sender. For example, if individuals contaminate the Earth's water, ultimately, they need to drink harmful and contaminated water.

A Wiccan thinks that his/her energy is never different from the power of the rest of life and the universe.

Focusing on intent

This concept of interconnectedness is the basis for the other Wiccan ethic, the Threefold Law. Whatever an individual sends out returns threefold. Generally, the law means that whatever you do or say-- unfavorable or favorable, bad or excellent-- will go back to you with three times the intensity. Some Wiccans believe that this belief applies just to words and actions, but others consist of thoughts.

Whatever that exists becomes part of one unbroken circle. So when a Wiccan decide to send energy, especially deliberate, powerfully directed energy during magic, that individual's essence:

- remains in the Self
- forms part of the power being sent out.
- It is in the result-- the energy that takes a trip through the circle of life, nature's web, and ultimately goes back to the sender.

That's why this particular ethic is referred to as the Threefold Law. The concept is, in some cases, called the Law of Return.

Observing the hex caution.

Non-Wiccan media and society tend to concentrate on hexing and cursing whenever the topic of Wicca or Witchcraft shows up. The truth is that many Wiccans do not take part in hexing, cursing, and other unfavorable acts.

Many Wiccans do engage in binding and banishing. The meaning of these concepts are as follow:

- Binding: A Wiccan may cast a spell designed to restrict the actions or activities of someone.

- Banishing: A Wiccan may order someone (or some energy) to be gone. To banish means to send someone or something away-- from the area, or possibly, back to the source.

Since they are negative forms of magic, many Wiccans avoid these practices. Some Wiccans use binding and eliminating as last options, when somebody or something positions a severe danger, usually to the neighborhood (for instance, a group of Wiccans may choose to bind a crook whois victimizing others.

A lot of Wiccans are exceptionally unwilling to take part in any form of harmful magic since they understand that their energy is never different from the heat of other individuals, and causing harm to others eventually leads to damage to the Self. They also are conscious that the failure to act to stop violence, to relieve suffering, and to end oppression is an offense of noble task and a betrayal of the neighborhood. So making use of extraordinary power remains a constant challenge for people of the Craft.

The colors of magic.

You might hear some people explain different forms of magic by referring to colors. The most common references are made to white magic and black magic or light and dark magic. Most likely, the terms black and white or light and dark magic dates back to a time in ancient human history when the night or the dark was associated with danger and fear. The daytime or light implied safety. These labels emerged from folklore, not modern Wicca, and lots of Wiccans don't use these characterizations today.

Usage of these terms perpetuates stereotypes about the Craft. Using the words black magic and white magic enhances society's false information and fear about the nature of magic. Besides, when someone states that she or he is a "white" or "great" Witch or Wiccan, the difference implies that others are "black" or "bad" Wiccans and witches. Society does not identify the fans of mainstream religious beliefs in this way. For example, Methodists aren't asked to state whether they are white or black Methodists, or good or bad Methodists.

These labels have been around for a very long time, and if you continue to study Wicca, you will undoubtedly encounter them. Here's a basic description of the significances for the colors of magic:

White magic is carried out for a definite purpose, a favorable result, or spiritual growth. A person conducts magic for him/herself or for somebody who has an understanding of the charm and has provided consent without any kind of coercion. Some Wiccans may carry out white magic for an uninformed individual (for instance, somebody who is seriously ill). Nevertheless, in those cases, the professional makes a general ask for the best possible outcome and then sends the radiant energy to Deity or out into nature (instead of sending the magic directly to the uninformed individual)—a lot of Wiccanspractice the white magic type.

The Black magic is any type of magic that is performed to push someone into doing something; is targeted at somebody against his/her will; is intended at somebody without his/her knowledge; or is made use of to produce a restrictive, undesirable, unethical, or objectionable outcome. Wiccans do not knowingly practice black magic.

Gray magic is mostly situational, and Wiccans differ on the right principles of its usage. Gray magic incorporates all of the elements of white magic with an addition: Gray magic includes magic for defense or security of the Self or others from danger, crisis, abuse, or threat. Often it is magically provided for the higher good. Numerous Wiccans think that they commit to stop wickedness, that they can't ethically disregard abuse, suffering, injustice, and soon. Gray magic permits a reaction for the greater good.

Green magic has numerous meanings. The term often explains magic performed on behalf of nature, or to help the Earth and its inhabitants. It can likewise suggest magic for healing or to ensure health. In some cases, the term is used for magic done to produce prosperity and abundance.

Some Wiccans likewise refer to blue, red, yellow, orange, or purple magic, but the true meanings of these terms vary.

CHAPTER SEVEN

LivingWiccanToday

Wiccans may have some distinct practices, and they deal with some different challenges. However, the average Wiccan is a sharp contrast to the stereotypes that lots of people still hold. This chapter offers you a glimpse into Wiccan lives and answers the question, "What's it like to be Wiccan?"

Taking a Snapshot of Contemporary Wicca

Who are Wiccans? Media representations of Wiccans have become more considerate for many years. However, the TV and film images probably do not show the lives of average Wiccans.

In truth, no one truly knows how lots of Wiccans are, who they are, and what sort of lives they lead. Wicca does not have large institutions that can supply this aggregate information. Wicca is a spirituality of little, loosely linked groups (although the Internet may be changing that fact by reinforcing the Wiccan neighborhood). Wicca does not have organized leadership or a centralized organization.

Lots of people declare that Wicca is the fastest-growing religion in America; however, no difficult data exists to prove this claim. Studies by several non-Wiccan groups, the growth of the Wiccan presence on the World Wide Web, and the increase in Wicca-related book sales support the concept that the variety of Wiccans is increasing. Also, records suggest that attendance at Pagan festivals is high and probably growing. Celebrations are events that typically occur in a rural setting at the very same time each year. They usually last for a weekend, or maybe several days. Festivals differ in size, but some draw numerous individuals. They offer Pagans a chance to connect socially and to exchange details about beliefs and practices.

Common sense suggests that Wicca is altering in addition to growing. The early individuals in the Wiccan revival are now middle-aged, and numerous have children. Dr. Helen Berger argues that the participation of entire households motivates Wiccans to develop companies and churches that will assist Wicca to expand and endure as a religion. Dr. Berger recommends that Wiccan parents want the faith to be deemed genuine by society so that their kids won't suffer persecution for their beliefs. Nevertheless, keep in mind that the population of the Berger study was small (approximately 2,000 people from several customs, consisting of Wicca) and self-selected (significance that individuals were not randomly selected, and they volunteered to respond). These respondents might or may not represent Wicca as a whole.

Out of fear of persecution and desire for privacy, many Wiccans lead extremely low-profile lives. Numerous do not divulge their affiliation with Wicca to outsiders. They go to work or school. They get back, cook dinner, see some TV, and go to sleep. They participate in PTA conferences and little league video games. They go to the motion pictures. They do read lots of books—the average Wiccan appearances and lives practically like anybody else.

Keeping Silent or Telling the World: The Wiccan Dilemma

Some people carefully hide their beliefs and never inform others about their involvement in Wicca, not their families, not their good friends, and not even their employers. Such people hide their altars, keep their books hidden in drawers rather than displaying on racks, and discover a reason to leave in a rush when people start discussing religion. They just share their beliefs with like-minded Wiccans, and often without anyone at all.

Other individuals, from the minute they experience Wicca, begin informing everybody they understand about the fantastic new world that they have found. They stack books on their friends, they hang pentacles in their cubicles at work, and they wear vibrant T-shirts happily displaying their devotion to Wicca. They're happy, and they want the world to know it.

Both Of These Positions Have a Benefit.

People who keep quiet aren't merely being paranoid. Most of the Wiccans are well versed in the long and harsh history of persecution against real and supposed Witches. Discrimination and abuse continue today worldwide.

Some people desire to keep quiet since they stress over being put in a position where they are required to reveal the names of other Wiccans. Also, some Wiccans are alarmed by the escalating usage of technology to gather and expose personal information about people.

Quite reasonably, some Wiccans pick to limit the number of individuals who understand their faith and could cause the problem, or even put them in threat-- now or in the future. You should never ask someone directly whether he or she is a Wiccan or a Witch. Wait up until the info is offered. If a person mentions the topic in discussion, show that you are open-minded and responsive; however, wait on the person to confide in you. If others can hear your argument, and this advice goes double. Never, and I never suggest ever, "call out" anybody. Don't reveal to others that someone is Wiccan without very first getting approval in private. Please respect that some individuals wish to keep their religious beliefs to themselves.

Some Wiccans think about Wicca to be a mystery religion that must be kept secret from the public. A mystery religion is one wherein the Deity is exposed through individual experience. These occasions are concealed to preserve their power and significance. Likewise, according to this view, some things are the best-taught person to person and need not be revealed. Also, particular knowledge and strategies (magic, for instance) might be unsafe if used by individuals who have not had proper training or who might intend to hurt others.

Individuals who choose to freely share their beliefs also have some excellent factors for doing so. Individual empowerment, along with physical, emotional, and psychological strength, is common to Wicca. Some Wiccans feel that living in fear of discrimination or dispute is contrary to their beliefs and limits their capability to practice their religion. Being truthful and open about Wicca builds self- self-confidence, which in turn makes incredible work more reliable and makes the ritual more fulfilling.

Some Wiccans believe that keeping their spirituality concealed motivates persecution and puts Wiccans in more risk, not less. Numerous feel that rejecting their religion dishonors the Goddess and the God. They likewise think that silence dishonored the Witches and declared Witches who have been eliminated in the name of Witchcraft.

The majority of Wiccans, however, find themselves at a happy medium between these two extremes. Many share their beliefs with friends and family. A smaller number are open about their religious beliefs in the work environment. Everyone needs to determine his/her level of convenience.

Many individuals find Wicca to be liberating and joyous. In their enthusiasm for their brand-new religious beliefs, new Wiccans may be tempted to chatter on about their religion to anybody who will listen, without sizing up the situation or the individual.

Some Wiccan traditions encourage that newbies learn and train for 'a year and a day' before disclosing their participation in Wicca to their communities. (A day and a year is a current period in Wicca. The year-and-a-day method is to make sure that Wiccans prepare well and think about all effects before making significant changes in their lives.).

Spilling the magic beans to friends and family.

Although Wicca has its roots in ancient times and is older than many of the world's religious beliefs, the Wiccan revival is a reasonably current phenomenon. A lot of individuals practicing Wicca today were not born into religious beliefs. They come from the recognized mainstream religious beliefs, typically from Christianity. When.

Relative might feel dissatisfied, upset, betrayed, or terrified. In all fairness, these intense emotions are reasonable. The household may think that the new Wiccan has turned his or her back on God, and might now remain in danger of going to Hell or suffering other exiles from God, as well as being separated from the remainder of the household after death and for all of eternity.

Everyone can practice whatever faith satisfies his/her needs, and friends or family should bully no one. Brand-new Wiccans can ease their shift by attentively considering the question of who to tell about their interest in or dedication to-- Wicca. Everyone's neighborhood is various, with varying degrees of tolerance. Nevertheless, the following ideas might be helpful to a Wiccan who wishes to share his or her spirituality:

Be selective and use profundity. Telling your partner, your sibling, and your buddy about your interest or involvement in Wicca may be essential to you, but do you genuinely need to have the same discussion with your judgmental but frail 91-year-old grandpa, with whom you go to once a year at the retirement home 1,100 miles away?

Be clear about your motives. Why are you informing a specific friend or member of the family? Do you wish to be genuine and deepen your intimate bond with this individual? Or are you merely trying to shock or be defiant? The previous is an excellent reason; the latter is, maybe, immature.

Beware. People can be unpredictable. When I made my change in spirituality, a few of the individuals whom I believed would be hostile or afraid ended up being incredibly tolerant. Others, sometimes individuals I expected to be helpful, or a minimum of cute were unpleasant, cynical, or downright nasty. Know that if you reveal your involvement in Wicca, you run the danger of alienating people who are necessary to you.

Weigh the threats of disclosure against what you stand to gain. If you decide to talk about your spirituality, pick the moment sensibly. Do not talk about the issue during a crisis. Select a time when you are calm and unhurried. You might even wish to compose down what you want to say so that you can provide your beliefs and without stress and anxiety. Focus on the favorable and attempt to alleviate the other individual's worries and concerns. Be respectful of his/her opinions; however, remain clear about the truth that you have every right to pick your faith.

Venturing out: Wicca in the work environment.

Choosing whether to be open about Wicca in the office is a huge choice that can have significant monetary repercussions. If you are checking out Wicca or have made a dedication, think of the benefits and drawbacks of divulging your beliefs before you speak about your spirituality at your worksite. You will most likely find that the novelty subsides quickly, and co-workers will treat you the same as they continuously have. Be mindful of the potential disadvantage of coming out of the broom closet at work. Here are some examples of bad things that can take place to good Wiccans:

Well, this one is apparent: You can get fired. Even in places where laws and business policies protect freedom of faith in the office, an employer who has strong opinions against Wicca might end you and mention other factors. Even if your immediate supervisor is open-minded and tolerant, your manager's boss might not be. Or the boss's discrimination might be more subtle. You may be passed over for promos or find your work under more examination. In some cases, you could submit a lawsuit; however, legal recourse is pricey, time-consuming, and seldom successful.

If you are in a service or an occupation that makes you dependent on clients or customers for your livelihood, understand that any disclosure about Wicca might threaten your sales or your relationships with clients. Depending on the nature of your service and your location, you might end up being the target of a boycott.

Be prepared to deal with co-workers who try to transform you. Other individuals may be interested and want to speak about your beliefs. Some of these conversations might be remarkably pleasant. Others might not be.

On the flip side, you may discover that a few of your colleagues avoid you, or perhaps avoid you. Associates may display hostility or worry. Depending on your office, the stigma might be long-term or temporary.

Wiccans-- specifically women-- have been stereotyped as being sexually promiscuous, uninhibited, and unrestrained. Whether this uses to you or not, the assumption can trigger issues at work in the kind of unwanted advances and even harassment.

The Benefits Of Being Open About Your Spirituality:

However, the scenario isn't all bad. The following are a few of the benefits of being open about your spirituality:

Some employers enable Wiccans the very same privileges as individuals of other faiths. Your employer might let you take off time on Wiccan holy days. Or you can work out for crucial days off; for example, you can offer to cover for your colleague on Good Friday if your colleague takes your place on Beltane.

You don't need to lie or avoid discussions that involve religion or spirituality. In a workplace where individuals are close and frequently share info about their personal lives, lying about or concealing your beliefs can get messy and tiresome.

When people know someone who is Wiccan, they are less most likely to think and promote stereotypes about Wiccans. Being open enables you to construct excellent will for Wicca and lead the way for others if you act morally and honorably.

Living outside of the mainstream needs guts. Having the stability, to be honest about your beliefs and face personal attacks can be empowering. The strength and self-confidence that you develop can serve you well in other areas of your life.

Wicca motivates individuals to live their lives with courage and stability. The next section offers a take a look at the sometimes distinct Wiccan approach to life and its passages.

Dancing the Circle of Life: Wiccan Passages.

Like everybody else, Wiccan lives are differentiated by passages: birth, adolescence, falling in aging, death, and love. Like individuals of every religion and culture, Wiccans engage in rituals, events, and rites to mark these happy or solemn celebrations. The following areas describe how Wiccans come and distinguish to terms with life's remarkable minutes.

Naming or Wiccaning of a child.

When a child comes into a Wiccan household, by birth or adoption, Wiccans might hold a ceremony to call the kid and place her or him under the protection of the Goddess and God, as well as the Wiccan community. The vast majority of Wiccans do not consider this to be a commitment or initiation of the kid into Wicca. It is more of an open event. The routine is simple and ordinarily short; however, it varies according to tradition. Non-Wiccans are generally complimentary to go to. Usually, a Priestess or Priest commands the ritual. Often a circle is cast. The rite typically includes the list below elements (the order might differ):.

- The kid is welcomed. He or she exists or presented to the Deity and the community.
- The kid is given his/her name.
- The selected Deity is asked to protect and bless the child.
- The community is asked to bless the child and safeguard. In some cases, each witness to the rite offers a one-sentence true blessing
- .The kid might be shown images of the forefathers, and the ancestors might be asked to bless the kid. The kid might be introduced to living relatives.
- All the guests take pleasure in wine (or juice) and cakes.

The rite ends, and the event is frequently followed by a party with feasting and the opening of gifts for the child. The Naming event is to show love and assistance for the kid and his or her household and is usually a warm and pleasing event.

Marking adolescence.

Coming-of-age rites that mark the age of puberty are not a universal practice in Wicca. Just like the rest of society, not all Wiccan moms and dads are entirely comfy with their kids' advance into sexual maturity, and adolescents might be too shy or ashamed to want this kind of event.

The rite is ending up being more typical for ladies. Some Wiccan women arrange rites of passage for their daughters in an attempt to balance the negative cultural conditioning that girls get about their bodies. For example, lots of young ladies are taught directly or indirectly that menstruation is a curse and a penalty for evil. No set structure exists for these coming-of-age rites, but most have the following in typical:

- For a lady, the rite generally occurs after she has her first menstruation. For a boy, the time is less plainly specified; however, it is usually around the time his voice deepens, and he starts to grow body hair.
- The rites haven't typically deemed a devotion or an initiation into Wicca. The age that kids reach puberty generally is thought about too young to make an educated life choice about religious beliefs.
- Guests are all of the very same sex as the teen going through the rite.

- The young individual understands about the rite ahead of time and understands the significance. Typically, she or he has the chance to take part in the preparation.

- Throughout the rite, the girl or young male is invited into adulthood and provided to the Goddess and/or God.
- Both pride and responsibility are worried during the ceremony.
- Typically, specific attendees offer brief little bits of recommendations to the adolescent.
- In some cases, the young adult is asked to symbolically part with some item from childhood, and after that, she or he is given something to represent the entry into adulthood. For some Wiccan families, this event is when the young person gets his or her first routine tools.

Aging with dignity: The wisdom of the Crone and Elder

One of the terrific disasters of modern-day civilization is how we treat the old. In this culture, individuals are valued based on their performance; that is, what they add to the system. The result is that children and the old are frequently cheapened and disrespected. Wiccan values reach back to the perfects of an earlier time, when all people had intrinsic worth, and the former were valued and respected.

Wiccans carry out Croning or Eldering rites to honor older members of the Craft who have acquired understanding, ability, and wisdom. To many in the Craft, an Elder is a guy or a woman who has reached his or her late 50s or older. Many Wiccans consider retirement age to be the time for an Eldering event. The term Crone typically applies to a female who has reached menopause. Crone is a regard to regard, not scorn. It is also the term for the 3rd aspect of the Goddess (Maiden, Mother, and Crone).

Croning or Eldering rituals are uncommon. The Wiccan revival wasn't fully underway up until the 1950s, so the number of older individuals in the Craft is restricted. As the Wiccan population ages, this ritual probably will end up being more prevalent.

Croning and eldering are rites of celebration and recognition. The focus is not just on the past accomplishment, however likewise the future capacity of the Elder or Crone.

Like coming-of-age rites, no set structure exists for this type of ritual. The celebration is geared to the person. Usually, a circle is a cast, and a Priest, Priestess, or other members of the community accompanies the Elder or Crone into the ring and presents him or her to the group of guests. The person's life and contributions are summarized. Frequently the Elder/Crone is given a gift signifying the celebration. Visitors are welcomed to speak, and after that, the Elder/Crone deals with the group. Celebration and gift-giving often follow the routine.

CHAPTER EIGHT

Wiccans Dealing with death

Everything in life, whatever in the cosmos, is made from one unbroken and eternal circle of energy. Energy has no start and no end. It can be changed, but it can not stop to exist. Truth is in ideal balance, a simultaneous cycle of creation and damage and birth, re-creation and death, and rebirth. This pattern repeats throughout the natural world, from the smallest of cells to the most huge of stars; everything is in an endless cycle of regeneration. The majority of Wiccans think that the very same concept holds real for human lives, and reincarnation is one of the most commonly held beliefs in Wicca.

Some Wiccans believe that after enough lifetimes or incarnations, the soul will reach a state of perfection and go back to the Divine Source.

Wiccans have varied concepts about the afterlife, and some are complicated. Some viewpoints take into account that time is not direct, and individuals might be living numerous lives at when. Some belief in Oversouls that branch off and manifest in multiple physical lives. Regardless of the subtleties, the majority of Wiccans do think in reincarnation.

Wiccans see death as a clean slate. They grieve similar to everybody else, but the unhappiness is from the pain of separation from the enjoyed one. If a Wiccan was open about his/her spirituality, the rites and the funeral service could be Wiccan, commanded by Wiccan clergy or a High Priestess or Priest. Wiccan memorial rituals differ according to custom, individual choice, and whether non-Wiccans exist. Usually, a circle is a cast, and the departed is kept in mind as in any considerate memorial service. Lots of Wiccans define that they desire to be cremated after death. However, Wiccans may pick various burial choices.

Ideally, the Wiccan has made arrangements for the disposal of his or her spiritual home, such as tools and the Book of Shadows. These individual

items might be damaged, buried with the Wiccan, or passed on to household or pals in the Craft. Fellow coveners or Craft pals should make sure that familiars and animals of the departed get a great house. (A familiar is an animal who has a psychic bond with a Wiccan.).

Infighting in the Witch Wars.

Wicca is in transition. It's acquiring legitimacy in the eyes of the general public. More Wiccans are venturing out of the broom closet and reaching out to one another. By all indications, Wicca is growing hugely. Wiccans are residing in a time of development and celebration of dialogue and exchange. The Goddess is re-emerging, and the world is rosy and bright for individuals of the Craft.

If you invest more than 10 minutes online going to Wiccan or Pagan Web websites, you'll see references to the Witch Wars.

The term is a little frightening and motivates stereotypical images of Witches hurling curses and lightning bolts at one another or Witches lined up on the field of battle, using middle ages garb and wielding long, decorated swords. This is not the case. The current Witch Wars are wars of words, but they do get pretty awful.

What are the Witch Wars?

In general, a Witch War is a verbal Internet fight between two or more people who call themselves Wiccans or Witches that occurs frequently.

Witch Wars generally begin little, in between people or small groups. The conflict spreads by way of gossip through the community (this chatter is in some cases called bitchcraft or Wicca). When the dispute reaches the media (most typically the Internet) and involves others in the neighborhood, it acquires momentum. Wiccans frequently are strong-minded individuals who think critically about issues. As a dispute gains public attention, others include their viewpoints to the fray, which draws more attention and greater media participation, which attracts others into the argument, and so on, till the result is a full-blown Witch War.

Witch Wars begin in numerous ways, consisting of the following situations:

- A single person or group questions the legitimacy of another individual's or group's beliefs, practices, training, or motivations. These arguments generally start with words such as, "You aren't a genuine Wiccan since ..." (See the following area for more on bad terms, such as fluff bunny and white lighter.).
- A person or group has a bad experience with another individual or group. Numerous Witch Wars begin with disappointments in covens. In some cases, the factor is simply coven politics: arguments over belief and practice, struggles for power, and breakdowns of communication (the very same issues that happen in other groups in society). Sometimes, the charge is more dangerous. One individual accuses another (or the group) of violating Wiccan principles, for example, implicating a member of sexual misconduct.

- Whatever the issue, the concern gets vented in public, usually on the Internet, and individuals take sides. Individuals exchange spoken fire until the debate is dealt with or burns out, one of the individuals leaves the field, or cooler heads prevail.

Among the considerable aspects contributing to the environment that creates Witch Wars is that, so a couple of covens exist. Lots of people are so desperate to find a coven that they end up among individuals with whom they aren't suitable. Individuals are thrown up who might have extremely various views about essential problems, such as management, ritual nudity, and so on. From this mix comes a difference that ends up being public and then spreads until another Witch War is at full speed.

A leader's integrity is perceived to be compromised.

Individuals view a particular leader to be in the Craft for his/her ego rather than spiritual reasons, for example, to wield power over others, to enjoy the adulation of fans, to get publicity, or to earn money. The leader's followers defend him or her; others publicly attack; war starts.

Wiccans argue over money.

Frequently, these disputes have to do with: The quality or authenticity of goods, services, training, or triggers is in concern. Are the owners of the local Pagan book shop supporting the community or exploiting it? (The vast bulk are invaluable resources to the community. However, some aren't.) Should a local coven charge people for Wiccan training? Should Wiccans claim that they can recover, and charge for this service?

- Rival Wiccan or Pagan organizations contend for donations. There are many useful organizations and insufficient Pagan dollars to support them. (Before you contribute, evaluate any Wiccan or other Pagan company naturally as you would any other group. Request a financial declaration and ask a lot of questions. A lot of are happy to accommodate your items.).

- Wiccans disagree about a company's plan. For instance, they may argue about whether or not to spend the neighborhood's cash to take a local case of discrimination to court.

Wiccans remain in conflict about what is and is not ethical habits.

This category encompasses a variety of issues. When, if ever, should Wiccans use magic for defense or defense? Should a Wiccan make claims about his or her ability to heal? When, if ever, is attempting to repair somebody without his or her knowledge and consent proper? Should Wiccans charge money for recovery? Should Wiccans charge money to teach the Craft? What kind of magic is acceptable?

The Internet seems to change how Wiccans and other Pagans interact with one another. Communication on the Internet, in email, chatroom, newsgroups, Web sites, and so on, often is confidential. Individuals feel freer to vent their feelings straight, impulsively, and with less tact than they would use during an in-person encounter. Sadly for the Wiccan neighborhood, name-calling and dispute have ended up being widespread online.

Who are white lighters and fluff bunnies?

Name-calling appears to have been raised to an art form on the Web. Names such as play an, fluff bunny, and whitelighter-- are used with varying degrees of intensity, from light-hearted fun to deep hostility. The significances of the terms depend on who utilizes them and in what context.

People new to the Craft go online and expect to discover Wiccans who respect all beings and live by the Wiccan Rede "An' it harm none, do what ye will" (Doreen Valiente, Pentagram, Volume One, 1964, released by Gerard Noel). Instead, sometimes they find Wiccans requiring conformity and spitting venom at one another. I include this area, not to motivate or excuse the usage of these words; however, so that beginners aren't blindsided by these habits; therefore, they understand the many terms that are being bandied about.

Fluff and light

Fluffy bunny and highlighter are the most typical terms that you may see on Wiccan Web sites and in publications. Initially, these bad terms were used by Wiccans and other Pagans about the New Age neighborhood. New Agers, in some cases, were deemed holding beliefs of little substance, and as being unrealistic, superficial, pointless, and, in many cases, materialistic. The paths of the New Agers, Wiccans, and other Pagans often crossed, and some

Wiccans and other Pagans rushed to separate themselves from what they considered as New Age fad. When the name-calling began, that's. The terms slowly progressed and were more often directed at Wiccans, whom others in the neighborhood felt were being New Age in their beliefs or practices.

A fluffy bunny or fluffy bunny is someone who is embracing or exploring Wicca for the wrong factors or in the incorrect methods, according to his or her critics. The term generally refers to individuals who do not understand or investigate the history, beliefs, or procedure that underlie the practice of Wicca. For some, Wicca is a trend; for others, it's a type of rebellion against society, the federal government, parents, or a mainstream church. Some are drawn into the tools, clothes, fashion jewelry, spells, public image, or media buzz; however, they have little interest in spiritual development. Some concentrate on particular misconceptions or assumptions about

Wicca and hold simplistic or biased views about Wicca and its history. Some are blindly devoted to one author or leader, however never research study and investigate further to get a deeper or wider point of view on the Craft. Some learned their Craft by watching popular television programs, such as Charmed, Sabrina the Teenage Witch, or Buffy the Vampire Slayer. All these folks have lots of fluff, according to their critics. (Playgan, rhymes with Pagan, is another term utilized for individuals who don't seem to take their Craft Seriously.).

A highlighter, a term in some cases utilized interchangeably with fluff bunny, is somebody for whom imagining white light (hence the name, highlighter) and sending good energy are enough for the practice of Wicca and the enhancement of the world. Whitelighters do not desire to take obligation for achieving particular acts in the Craft, typically because they don't wish to run the risk of doing any harm. They do not explore how Craftworks. They concentrate on joyous and positive routine, and mainly disregard significant issues worldwide. This term explains feel-good, delighted Wicca combined with New Age philosophy and practiced by people who don't have a clue, according to the critics who use this term.

The definitions of these terms vary, depending upon the context and the critic, but they are rarely used as a favorable or encouraging comment. (However, the unfavorable significance of whitelighter might be altering because of the popularity of the tv show, Charmed. On that program, a highlighter is a spiritual protector or guardian, and that meaning is working its way into general use.).

Sticks and stones.

The preceding are primary descriptions for these disparaging words. Their use has become much more widespread and isn't restricted to those descriptions. Wiccans often snap with these words in the following situations:

More knowledgeable members of the Craft judge the sincerity or integrity of new Wiccans or people exploring Wicca.

Some Wiccans and other Pagans call every newcomer a fluff bunny. (A a little more helpful term for someone new to Wicca or Paganism is newbie; the more respectful and respectful name is hunter.).

The generation space often fuels this division in the Craft. Older Wiccans usually charge that the younger ones just don't understand what times resembled when Wicca was harmful, deceptive, and hard to gain access to. The older generation developed modern-day Wicca in a world that was hostile to them, and some are afraid that the more new age will make modifications in the traditions that they worked so tight and risked a lot to develop. Some do not think that young Wiccans value the severity of the course. Members of covens (arranged little groups) judge solitaries.

(Wiccans who practice alone).

Many traditions (denominations or sects) of Wicca do not recognize as legitimate individuals who practice Wicca without being and joining a coven started into a formal custom, slowing Wicca's emergence as a spirituality that society recognizes as genuine. Witch Wars and name-calling enhance society's stereotypes of Wiccans as possibly dangerous individuals without any morals and principles.

If such internal disputes continue, efforts to get acceptance for Wicca in the courts, the workplace, and other institutions will take longer. It also implies that the children of Wicca are most likely to grow up dealing with persecution, discrimination, and public hostility instead of progressive approval.

The Wiccan community can, and does, interact to further shared objectives. Most Wiccans welcome new specialists and are more than willing to listen to others and discuss their own beliefs in a non- confrontational way. The secret for Wiccans is to transport the passion into enhancing the Craft, not into protecting specific positions or assaulting those of others.

CHAPTER NINE

Considering The Wiccan Path

Some Wiccans know intuitively that Wicca is best for them. From the beginning, they never question their choice of spiritual path. Others have a more analytical nature, and they analyze their religious decisions. Vigilance and uncertainty are very welcome in Wicca. Wicca supports questioning of authority.

Looking Inward

Many people have chosen to read this book just because they want information about Wicca and Witchcraft. If that's true for you, this area does not personally apply. If you mean to pursue a much more in-depth exploration of Wicca or you're moving towards making a dedication, make sure that you aren't drawn to Wicca for reasons that are unrelated to faith. If it is followed for purposes other than spiritual ones, the Wiccan knowledge will not be gratifying or transforming. If your response to any of the following questions is yes, take a while to reconsider your interest in Wicca:

1. Is somebody pressuring you to get involved in?

Wicca?

Wiccans support independence, free choice, and personal strength. They do not attempt to convert others. If somebody is trying to push you into participating in Wiccan activities or study, that individual is not a real Wiccan, and you may have to free yourself from such manipulation.

2. Are you angry at your previous religion, and you think that Wicca is the"opposite" of your former faith?

Many injustices have been done in the name of or under the guise of religion. Naturally, some people feel betrayed by religious organizations. You will be more efficient if you choose a religion for positive and genuine reasons.

3. Are you drawn to Wicca just because you view it to be counter-cultural, underground, or subversive?

The reality is that Wicca can be considered worthy of all these labels. However, Wicca is foremost and first a spirituality, not merely a method to rebel against your household, the government, or mainstream society.

4. Do you feel lonely and think that Wicca, specifically a coven, can function as a family and satisfy your requirements for companionship?

Many coveners do develop strong, close-knit bonds with one another. A reverence for Deity and a love of nature, not a desire to fulfill emotional needs, are the basis for a sound dedication to Wicca.

By the way, Wiccans do not cut their ties to household and good friends when they commit themselves to Wicca. They continue to support their relationships with individuals beyond Wicca.

5. Are you in the real sense, just searching for sex?

The concept that Wiccans and Witches engage in orgies as part of their rites is prevalent. This stereotype isn't real; sexual activity is not a part of standard Wiccan practice.

6. Are you brought in just to the image or the more remarkable aspects of Wicca, for instance, jewelry, robes, tools, or fancy routines?

The practice of Wicca is gorgeous, but the basis for Wiccan activities is to honor the Deity and commemorate the natural world.

7. Do you think that Wicca can provide you some secret power or details that can solve your problems, such as getting you out of debt, breaking an addiction, or healing your relationship with your partner?

The majority of people understand that it's not possible to point a finger or wiggle a nose to clean up your home right away, attract a mate, or conquer enemies. Some people do have the idea that Wicca can impart a secret power or expose some unearthly ancient knowledge.

It is a fact that Wicca is a spirituality of profound knowledge; its roots remain in the Old Religion, which reaches back countless years. Wicca can offer you tools for transforming your life (for example, details about healing or rituals for growth and empowerment).

It is also the truth that the practice of magic directs energy, which could enable you to make modifications in yourself and the world. However, nobody in Wicca can bestow upon you a word, beauty, or spell that unexpectedly puts an end to all your difficulties.

8. Speaking of television Witches, are you buying into the media buzz?

From Samantha to Sabrina to the siblings on Charmed, Witches have been continuously popular on television, but be assured that real-life Wicca isn't anything like television Witchcraft.

This section brings to light some nonreligious reasons that people might be brought in to Wicca and Witchcraft; the next article addresses some of the spiritual problems that people grapple with as they consider whether Wicca is ideal for them.

Asking the Big Questions.

How do individuals select their faiths? Some are born into a religion and never question their devotion to their childhood religious beliefs. Some claim to understand intuitively when they discover the religious beliefs or spirituality that is best for them. Others participate in a mission to find the perfect spiritual course. They discover their core values and concepts and then compare them to the mentors of different religions. The following are common or regular questions that people might ask themselves when they are attempting to define their beliefs:

- How do I wish to live? What is my purpose? What is most important to me?
- What type of interpersonal relationships do I desire to have?

- How do I wish to raise my children? How do I want to treat my parents?
- How do I desire to express my sexuality?
- How essential is money in my life? What am I happy to do to get it?
- What happens to me when I die? How do I prepare for death? Am I scared to die?
- How do I feel about the world? Do I desire to live fully in it? Change it? Escape it? Transcend it?
- How do I value other people around me?
- How should individuals treat the Earth?
- What is morality? What is evil? Does evil exist?
- Do I genuinely believe in a holy book or other doctrines?
- Who or what do I rely on when I am suffering?
- Do I believe in any Deity? How do I envisage Deity?

A lot of religions spell out the answers to these questions in detail. They have at least one holy book that deals with these problems. They also have churches or other organizations with leaders who interpret doctrine and counsel people about how to live.

Ideally, a person's core or significant values, beliefs, and principles agree with the mentors of his/her chosen faith, suggesting that he or she concurs with the religion's leaders and teaching.

Wicca does not have a teaching or holy book that Wiccans must follow, nor does it have leaders who require that people live a specific way. Wicca is a spiritual path with some core principles and objectives that most Wiccans hold in common. Their responses show the core concepts of Wicca when Wiccans address these huge life questions. Wiccans select this spiritual path since they share the standard Wiccan ideas about life, the world, and Deity.

Wiccan Principles

A Wiccan can decline several of the principles that a lot of Wiccans hold in common. No authority decides who is and is not a legitimate Wiccan. However, it's doubtful that someone can be pleased or reliable in Wicca if he or she declines the bulk of the following core principles:

- **Immanent Deity**

Practically all Wiccans think Creatively. Wiccans can have drastically different understandings of Deity. Many Wiccans define Deity in both the male and female aspects, that is, the Goddess and God. The principle of immanence is central to Wicca. Immanence implies that.

Divine being is right here, right now, and is all-present on the planet, instead of transcendent (over or beyond the world). People originate from and belong to the Divine energy, and Deity is within everyone. A Wiccan's crucial spiritual intent is to grow in his/her relationship with Divinity.

Interconnection

Wiccans believe that everything is interconnected. All of human existence is an unbroken circle of energy, and everything is combined into one living organism. Nature is a manifestation of Deity, and individuals commit to regard, safeguard, and protect the natural world.

Love for Community

For Wiccans, the word "community" incorporates all the natural world, consisting of all people. Since it is a manifestation of Deity, Wiccans feel an individual responsibility to respect and serve the community. It was harming, even by neglect or apathy breaches, Wiccan principles. Respecting and serving the community means working to end any condition that causes harm, consisting of poverty and oppression. Wealth ought to not be valued over people, the Earth, and its inhabitants. Sexuality is a symptom of and a gift from Divinity. Therefore it ought to be celebrated, taken part in carefully, and never used to cause damage.

Since Deity is within everybody, all people are equal, and they should not be seen differently based on race, ethnic culture, sex/gender, sexual preference, class, education, or beliefs. Wiccans are not perfect, and prejudice exists in Wicca, as in every other section of society. Still, bias breaches Wiccan principles and ethics, as does any type of violence or abuse.

Life and the afterlife.

Wiccans think that whatever that exists is an unbroken circle of energy. Energy has no beginning and no end. Life is a cycle of rebirth, birth, and death. Based on this conception, many Wiccans believe in some type of reincarnation, although the information differs. Lots of think that, upon death, the soul or the awareness goes to the Summerland, a location of peace and natural charm that is located in non-physical, non-ordinary reality. The soul or consciousness might rest in Summerland, review the life that has just passed, and decide whether to reincarnate or explore other possibilities.

Nearly all Wiccans agree that lifestreams from the Deity, so life is not to be simply endured or suffered. The Wiccan intent is to honor Divinity by living life to its fullest potential-- not to go beyond experience, but to revel in it.

Wiccan Ethics.

Wicca doesn't force individuals to abide by commandments and laws. The Threefold Law and the Wiccan Rede are widely accepted in Wicca. They are guidelines by which each Wiccan constructs his/her code of principles. Wiccans quibble amongst themselves about the nuances, nevertheless, if somebody thinks in general to the ethical requirements in this area, she or he most likely would not be comfortable in Wicca.

Self-direction and individual obligation

Wicca is a spirituality, not a religious belief. It is based on experience, not doctrine. No holy book or leader tells people what to do and when, or offers forgiveness for sin. Wiccans decide on an individual basis how to live, how to praise, and how to practice Wicca. Lots of people discover this lack of structure liberating; others might feel insecure and directionless.

Protection of personal privacy and restriction on proselytizing

Privacy and confidentiality are essential in Wicca. The individual chooses whether to be open about his/her spirituality and if and when to reveal such info. No one may expose the identity of another Wiccan. To do so could jeopardize the person's friendships, career, kid custody, and so on.

Wiccans do not proselytize (meaning that they don't try to convert others to their religious beliefs). They feel that proselytizing is unneeded; individuals who are drawn to Wicca look for and discover others of like mind.

Knowing for Sure

How does someone understand for sure whether he or she is Wiccan? If you ask Wiccans this question, you may get actions like these:

" I feel in my bones.".

" It seemed like I was coming home.".

" I feel the existence of the Goddess." "I got an indication from nature.".

These are all truthful actions, but they aren't efficient to somebody who is examining Wicca from the outside.

Since it is based on individual experience, Wicca is tough to get a handle on. Wicca is a spirituality of exploration and discovery, instead of church services and doctrine. Wiccans discover their connection to Deity. They feel the presence of, or they interact with, the Goddess and God. They start to feel a deep kinship with the universe. They may begin to pay attention to and discover significance in synchronicities (coincidental occasions that seem associated) occurring in their lives. Their understandings change, and they end up being conscious of nature's cycles and patterns. They typically find themselves gaining wisdom from the natural world, including animals.

Wiccans typically do not believe in coincidence. They live their lives open up to interaction from Deity and in tune with nature. Feeling the existence of Divinity and the bond with the natural world affirms their choice of Wicca as their spiritual course.

Taking the First Step

A lot of Wiccans would recommend that you don't hurry headlong into it if you feel drawn to Wicca. Your spiritual journey will be a lot more changing and fulfilling if you take some time and exercise your sensations and beliefs. Start gradually. Do you believe in the Goddess and God? Begin hoping regularly and support the Divine relationship.

Do not get caught up in attempting to work magic immediately. You might not get the wanted outcome if you do not build a structure of understanding.

Focus on natural phenomena, such as solar and lunar eclipses. Invest some time in nature and let yourself be completely present and open. Put ordinary fret about profession or household aside for a time, and concentrate on your environments. Feel the interconnection of all living things and the existence of the Goddess and the God. That is the very best possible intro to Wicca.

CHAPTER TEN

Principles Of Wiccan Belief

Like most real kinds of spirituality, Wicca creates complacency and stability within the follower. This sense of balance brings a guarantee for the future. When this sense of security is integrated with a real love for deity, the deep space of the soul is filled, and genuine assurance is found.

Among the most exceptional functions of all religious beliefs are beliefi.ebelief in deity, sacred bible, and ritual customs. Ideas form the nucleus of all spiritual systems. They are the source from which the faith thrives and grows. Without strong beliefs, no teaching can weather the tides of time.

Since Witchcraft is a child with lots of fathers and the offspring of a thousand complaints, it is hard to place the beliefs of one tradition above another. No one knows for sure where the majority of Wicca's doctrines come from, and to make complex matters, the majority of modern Wiccans often disagree when it comes to religious issues.

There is something that most Pagans and Wiccanswill agree on: The Principles of Wiccan Belief. These principles form the foundation of modern Wiccan belief, much as the Ten Commandments do for the Christian religion. The concepts, which follow, were embraced by the Council of American Witches at their 1974 spring meeting in Minneapolis. Many Wiccans still cling to these principles, although the council disbanded soon after its spring meet that year.

Conventional Coven Policy

The word "coven" generally summons visions of individuals all worn black, wildly dancing around a bubbling cauldron. While this picture is not always without merit, it is not the amount total of Witchcraft or the Wiccan religion.

Many Witches choose to stay solitary (that is, to work alone), some join covens, generally made up of thirteen individuals, including a leader. The number thirteen is considered lucky just because it can't be divided against itself. This is, however, the suitable, and not the norm. The majority of groups have far fewer members.

One of the very first things a new member is given upon signing up with a coven is a list of tenets or coven laws. The coven members have drafted these laws to maintain order. They are generally based upon an act of courtesy and common sense, two things many people appear to forget when feelings are involved.

The Laws

1. Each tradition or group in Wicca has its own processes and beliefs. Each must follow according to its path. So long as it hurts none and respects the spirit of deep space, all traditions will be considered as equally legitimate under the God and Goddess.

2. Our members believe there is a supreme force that created and maintained deep space and represented itself through the myriad of universal goddesses and gods. We acknowledge these

gods and goddesses as entire and complete unto themselves and equal unto each other.

3. On our part, we do not fear to have a lady bring in a female, nor a guy bring in a male. It is better to have a wise instructor of the same sex than a fool of the opposite.

4. We see Wicca as a response, not a reason to prevent that which takes effort or might be emotionally hurtful.

5. For those who look for the initiation, it must be kept in mind that the introduction is an occurrence within the heart. The ceremony is just its restatement before the gods and those who represent them.

6. Within any organization, there should be a leader or several leaders. In Wicca, we recognize that there is no such thing as an ideal High Priestess or High Priest. The imperfections of the leaders should not be the reason for a disorder, but rather for love, tolerance, and understanding.

7. When there should be a cessation of friendship, there comes a time in every family or coven. What one might avoid saying to a good friend or liked one, one may be forced to say as a High Priestess or High Priest. Discipline is one such responsibility.

8. You should remember you will never have the power of the instructor who tutored you. This does not mean that you won't

ever have the same amount of energy as those who came in the past.

Power is not an ability, and your capability may surpass all others. Power is the ability to demand respect. You will never have the regard due to your instructors. Need your own by controlling your ability.

9. Thinking of hurting is not like working to cause discomfort. Each step may be accomplished with little force of will, but with greater strength of will, both can be prevented.

10. Those with knowledge and capability need not show it—those who fear their ability to fear themselves. Worry has no location within the Craft of the Wise.

11. Express only that which you know. Work only within your world of schedule. Leave the fools unto themselves, and look for people with the truth in their hearts. Don't allow their words or actions lead you but instead, seek to their works and deeds.

12. Observe, listen, and reserve judgment. For till the silver is weighed, who knows the weight.

13. Always treat others as you would want to be dealt with. Keep in mind that evil begets evil, but good begets pleasure and joy.

CHAPTER ELEVEN

Deity: The God And Goddess

Wicca is an extremely individualized religion, in which each individual selects his or her divine beings to worship. Usually, the supreme being is thought about to be a genderless energy source like The Force in the Star Wars trilogy. This force is described as the All, and it consists of several elements of deep space. These aspects are shown in the manly and feminine energies of nature, which are shown in the form of different gods and goddesses existing in the world.

Individuals getting interested in Wicca mostly question just who or what the Pagan gods are. Are the images of the human mind developed by our forefathers? Are they stereotypical images of the cumulative human mind? Are they cosmic forces that antedate the human race? The response is not an easy one and should be discovered for oneself through training and experience.

This specific liberty to pursue and contemplate that which originates from within is what makes Witchcraft such an exceptional experience. There is no pressure to embrace another individual's concept or principle of divine being. There is no one, true, best, and only way. Everyone is considered to be accountable for his/her spiritual development, advancement, and relationship with deity.

The God

Like all divine beings, God has many faces. He looks like the radiant, fantastic, and illuminating Sun of Righteousness. To all those who indulge in the practice of Wicca, God exists as a sign of potency, the fertilizing, and regrowing force of nature. He personifies all that is masculine, powerful, and powerful.

The god's most apparent and dominant characteristic is his capability to regrow. His countenance might change with time and culture; he continually returns to live and die for the land he enjoys. He has been known as Osiris, Tammuz, and Adonis. He has manifested as the unconquered Sun or compassionate rescuer Mithra and Helios. Whatever his version, he is continuing the potentate of strength, authority, and power- and the final judgment before the eviction of the Goddess.

The Sun Cod

In Wicca, the existence of the divine is viewed in all the different aspects of nature. One of the most appreciated natural phenomena is that of the sun. This radiant ball of fire offers light, produces life, and promotes recovery. In addition to its timekeeping qualities, a crucial aspect of life, it has long represented God.

The Sun God was believed to rule the sky, and all that moved below it during the daytime. He presided over time, war, fertility, agriculture, and the regeneration of life. In the Romano-Celtic stage of Old Europe, the sun god was seen as being in a continuous fight with the forces of evil and darkness. To support the Sun God in the struggle against the powers of darkness, people worshiped him throughout morning routines. It was thought that these routines would provide him strength and help revive his brilliance each day.

The Harvest God

The god of greenery administered over the farming community as the child and lover of the great Mother Earth. He was highly personified in the Middle East as Tammuz, in Egypt as Osiris, and throughout ancient Europe as Dionysus and Adonis.

In ancient myths, the returning and passing away god, as portrayed in harvest rites, offered a way of redemption. To end up being part of his mystery custom was to guarantee for oneself a location within the structure of the afterlife.

To a lot of our ancestors, the harvest was a time of both event and mourning. The abundance of grain and white wine were cause for excellent delight.

The ancient misconceptions of Tammuz and Ishtar, Aphrodite and Adonis, and Isis and Osiris, best communicate this compelling drama of return, death, and life - all products of the harvest process. This cycle of growing, dying, and returning was the structure of the Pagan secrets that precede Christianity. It is also the main focus of most modern Wiccan customs.

When dealing with Wiccan gods, remember the main characteristics: The Sun God represents beauty, youth, and knowledge.

The Goddess

After centuries of exile, the goddess has made her way back to her land, people, and position as the personification of womanly perception and dominion. She is the Mistress of Magic; she is all that is charm and bounty. What the God inaugurates, the Goddess understands.

The Goddess is the instinctive and intuitive side of nature. Her incredible powers of shift and transformation radiate o

+like bright beams of celestial light, for she is the mystery and magic. Below her full, round moon she has been, and still is, conjured up as Arianrhod, Diana, and Hecate by those seeking her favors.

The Moon Goddess.

The moonlit the way for early human beings. The moon glowed in the night sky. Its light helped in guiding tourists, warriors, and hunters securely through the dark and back to their tribes.

As our ancestors sought to the heavens, they saw how the moon waxed and subsided, how the night was turned into day, spring into summer, and summer season into the winter season. They saw the seas ups and downs, plants come up with grain, and life burst forth from the womb. The Great Goddess highly worshiped in Old Europe became corresponded with the moon, in whose great light she was reflected. As the moon subsided and waxed, so did the Goddess' significant power and authority.

When the moon reached its full, pregnant magnificence, it was viewed as the Mother. Here we discover the nurturer, the provider of life and bringer of death, the Goddess's most potent, and indeed most revered stage. This was the time of excellent fertility and increased psychic awareness. It was a time typically set aside to visualize and formulate physical desires.

The subsiding moon saw the decrease of light and was connected with the Crone, who signified the manifestation process and was combined with knowledge. What was developed on the complete moon was realized during the waning moon. This was also a time of consideration and awareness of personal achievements.

As soon as the moon completes its three significant stages, it passes into a period of transition, referred to as the New Moon. This 3-day duration was and still is, considered the time of the Enchantress or Temptress-a time of terrific mystery and magic.

The Mother Goddess.

The Mother Goddess is a highly complicated figure, also the most influential figures within the Wiccan religion. She is the embodiment of feminine appeal, fertility, and the ability to support. In the old Pagan times, the Mother Goddess ruled over the fecundity of people and animals.

To our Pagan ancestors, the Mother Goddess enjoyed both was and feared. She was the tranquil benefactor in charge of regrowth, life, and fertility. As the Great Mother, she came up with experience, and as the Terrible Mother, she ruled over death and destruction.

Throughout ancient Europe, the Mother Goddess embraced a vast array of activities. Besides her association with fertility, she was likewise the embodiment of maturity and abundance. To portray these qualities, images of the Mother Goddess were endowed with large breasts, inflamed bellies, and full butts.

The principle of nurturing, with its ability to transcend the harsh realities of life and express genuine love, brings lots of people to the Goddess of Wicca. Their connection to the potential of the symptom process is reawakened once they are embraced by the Mother Goddess. When this takes place, people become able to get in touch with their nurturing potential, which develops spiritual maturity.

Picked Wiccan Goddesses.

Brigid: Celtic Triple Goddess. She is the embodiment of poetry, prophecy, and motivation. Brigid has initially been a fire, and the sun goddess understood as Brigid of the Golden Hair. Since her connection with the shooting, Brigid was associated with motivation and the art of smithcraft. Brigid was also a crucial fertility goddess. She was called on throughout birth to protect the mom and the child. Brigid's signs include the spindle, flame, well, ewe/lamb, snake, bell, and milk.

Cerridwen: Cerridwen, which is associated with Astarte or Demeter, is referred to as the mother goddess of the moon and grain. She is specifically known for her fearsome death totem, a white, corpse-eating plant. Cerridwen' s harvest events express her ability to both take and provide away life. Her symbols consist of the cup, sow, cauldron, and hound.

Diana (The Roman Moon Goddess): She was the patroness of hunters and guardians of the forest where her spiritual grove existed near Aricia. Diana's signs consist of the weapon, shoes, beautiful weapons, the dog, and the stag.

Demeter: Greek Earth Mother. As the goddess of vegetation, she was the creator of agriculture and the civic rite of marital relationships.

Isis (The Egyptian Mother Goddess): Isis is the personification of the Great Goddess in her aspect of maternal devotion. Isis was probably the biggest goddess in Egypt and was worshiped for more than 3,000 years. Her impact was not confined to Egypt and infected Greece and the Roman Empire. Isis was the female concept of nature and, for that reason, a goddess of a thousand names. Isis's signs include the Thet (knot or buckle), scepter, cup, horns, girdle, mirror, and snake.

Rhea (The Cretan Mother Goddess): Her name probably means Earth, and she was typically portrayed as a huge, magnificent lady surrounded by animals and small, subservient human males. Rhea was included in the Greek myth as a Titan, one of the second generation of deities. She was regarded as the goddess of the living earth. Rhea's symbols include the torch, double ax, brass drum, and trees bearing fruit.

The Morrigan (The Celtic Triple Goddess): The Morrigan is the dreadful hag goddess of the Celtic legend. She bears some relationship to the Furies and Valkyries of Norse Myth. She looks like a triple goddess of battle and illustrates the extreme, unrelenting warrior side of the Celtic soul. The Morrigan's s signs include the raven, crow, fight spear, shield, and ax.

When dealing with Wiccan goddesses, keep in mind primary attributes: Moon Goddess represents spiritual illumination and is the essence of magic and secret; Mother Goddess represents the sensual/nurturing side of the womanly nature and is filled with grace; and Triple Goddess exemplifies knowledge, seductiveness, and enchantment.

Seasons of the God and Goddess.

Wicca, like all mystery traditions, relies significantly on symbolism. When an individual sees a symbol, his or her consciousness is automatically elevated to a world of higher understanding. Religious art, objects, and charts are used to develop a bridge between the conscious and unconscious minds. They both expose and veil particular truths and facts according to each person's level of understanding.

The Seasons of the God and Goddess chart, which follows, is an excellent example of symbolic illustration. Taking a look at the table, one instantly grasps the relationship between time and divine being. Whereas the Goddess keeps a controlled and restrained position within the seasonal cycle, the God is more independent, less confined, and not as directly included with cyclic modification. It is typically accepted that feminine energy is more influential and involved with the cycles of nature than masculine energy is, even though the latter does have a dominating impact.

CHAPTER TWELVE

Introduction To Witchcraft

What is Witchcraft?

Those who identify as Wiccans and those who are Witches have differences of viewpoint relating to the term "Witchcraft." While not every Witchcraft is considered to be "Wiccan," the words "Wicca" and "Witchcraft" are frequently used interchangeably.

Some Wiccans argue for a difference between what they consider to be spirituality-based worship ("Wicca") and more "secular" practice (" Witchcraft"), however, mostly, the two are intertwined enough that the difference isn't especially beneficial.

With due regard to Wiccans who recognize a distinction, the term "Witchcraft" will be used in this book to explain the necessary activities found in rituals practiced by Wiccans and non-Wiccan Witches alike. Because some Wiccans do not practice magic and do not consider themselves Witches, the term "Witch" in this section of the book is used to refer those who both adopt Wiccan practices in some kind or another and practice magic as part of their religion.

Witchcraft is the set of practices and beliefs used by Witches in ritual and spellwork. Often, beautiful work is added to the Sabbat and Esbat events observed by covens and solitary Witches, though spell might be used by itself on other occasions. In reality, many Witches consider themselves to be continuously "practicing" their Craft in their every day lives through using meditation, amazingly charged meals and drinks, color choices in clothing and jewelry, nighttime candle routines, and other apparently "small" enactments of magic. The more one is in tune with the rhythms and energies of the natural world, the more "wonderful" one's life will feel and seem, and this relationship with the cycles of life is deepened throughout one's life through study and practice.

"Magic" is a word used for the phenomena that happen when people knowingly take part in the co-creative forces of the Universe, by using the subtle energies of nature to trigger the necessary change in their truth.

People may use magic, or "the Craft" as it is frequently called, for many purposes. This often includes spells, appeals, and other operations for what could be called "personal gain," such as a new job or improvements in a love relationship. However, the Craft is also used to work for benefits to one's household, neighborhood, and even to individuals around the world. A coven might use an Esbat ritual as a chance to send out beneficial recovery light to victims of a natural disaster. What the Craft is not used for is anything that would cause harm to another person or other living beings, even unintentionally. Our dreams can often be manipulative when it concerns how they impact other individuals, even when we do not understand it. For that reason, routine and spellwork frequently consist of safeguards versus unintentional abuse of magical energy, such as the phrases "for the good of all" and "harm to none"-- taken from the Wiccan Rede. Keeping this idea in the leading edge of one's mind is essential, especially in light of another basic tenet of Witchcraft: the Threefold Law.

The Threefold Law

Also called "The Rule of Three" and "The Law of Return," this principle specifies that everything witches send out into the Universe as intent, whether negative or positive, will come back to them three times as fantastic. While some Witches don't go with this particular belief, it is usually conjured up as a suggestion that incredible power should be used just for good, and never in the spirit of damage or manipulation.

Magic and Science

Many modern authors on Witchcraft have explained the relevance of discoveries in the physical sciences that seem to determine what Witches have always known to exist: a cooperative relationship between mind and matter.

This relationship can be viewed from numerous angles and is probably not entirely understood by anybody. Still, its presence is glaring to professionals of magic as well as other mind/thought-based disciplines that cause favorable modification in one's life.

The standard worldview of the majority of Western society for the past couple of centuries has held that truth is chaotic and inflexible, developed by forces beyond human control. It has likewise held that the mind is not a physical entity, and is separate from what we believe of as "matter." What Witches understand, and what science has begun to discover, is that reality is versatile, and is co-created by and with everything in it, consisting of the mind.

The power of an idea has been brightened in many books and videos about the "Law of Attraction," a "New Age" subject that has just recently found popularity among mainstream audiences, celebrities, and even company professionals. The Law mentions that ideas draw in experiences that reinforce them, so that home on negative situations can keep them in place, while concentrating on favorable experiences produces improved circumstances. Altering one's thoughts is more complicated than it may appear, of course, which is perhaps why a lot of information and advice regarding the Law of Attraction is currently readily available.

The Hermetic Principles

Witchcraft can be stated to employ the Law of attraction in a sense, though magic can be much more intricate than just focusing one's ideas on a preferred outcome. It might be more accurate to state that Witches use routines, tools, words, and presents from the natural world to improve and broaden their deal with the Hermetic Principles.

The Hermetic Principles date back to late antiquity and have notified Western religious, philosophical, esoteric, and clinical ideas. They have intriguing parallels in modern physics, consisting of quantum mechanics and string theory, and explain the method reality operates on a subatomic level, where all product things are composed of energy and radiate energy. Lots of Witches have been watching excitedly as the scientific understanding of the makeup of deep space unfolds to validate what ancient observers understood.

There are seven Hermetic Principles, which are typically referred to in most discussions of magic. One of the most emphasized is the Law of Correspondence, which mentions that what is correct on the macrocosm is likewise real on the microcosm. This suggests that every particle of matter contains all others-- and that linear time on the physical aircraft represents just one dimension in the ultimately spaceless and classic overall Universe. Another way of stating the concept is "as above, so below, as listed below, so above." The more enormous planes of existence influence the lower planes of presence, and vice versa. As microcosms of the Universe, we can glean info from the far-off past, view pictures of the future through divination, and alter our reality.

A widely-reported and recent research study discovered that the laws governing the development of the Universe share substantial resemblances to the development of both the human brain and the Internet.

Just as every particle of matter consists of all others, matter and energy all include info at their the majority of basic level. The Universe, eventually, is mental at its highest level, which is the underlying innovative force of all things. We understand that all the developments, developments, and adjustments in our human history started as concepts. Witches also understand that ideas can affect the Universal mind, and this is part of why focused intent in ritual is essential.

The Law of Vibration holds that whatever remains in continuous movement, and that absolutely nothing is at rest. This applies even to relatively sturdy physical things such as tables and chairs-- they have vibrations than we just can't view with the human mind-matter is comprised of energy, which is essentially a force moving at a specific wave. The parallel with animism deserves noting here, as animists believe that whatever is alive. If a quality of being "alive" is to be in motion, then the animists have been appropriate the whole time.

The nature of colors as light moving at various rates of vibration is particularly helpful in Witchcraft, as each color's frequency has particular attributes ideal for specific purposes. We frequently associate love with the colors red and pink, for instance, and it ends up that these colors resonate with energies in the body that promote loving sensations. Therefore, these colors, when used in spellwork to bring love into one's life, both communicate that information appropriately to the Universe and connect it to the Witch's energy field. Naturally, like all things, colors can have their disadvantages. The high vibration of the color red can also overstimulate and activate unpleasant feelings. Color treatments utilizing the Chakra system and meditation techniques often seek to stabilize out-of-whack fluctuations in the body, and colors can

Be used amazingly in much the same method.

Comprehending systems like the Hermetic Principles and the Law of Attraction can be useful in increasing one's success in magic. However, a thorough grounding in them is not completely necessary. And it's valuable to remember that no matter how effective the intentions for magic might be, outcomes may be restricted by the unknown universal truths of the real and more magnificent airplanes-- sometimes we're just not implied to get precisely what we want at a particular time. It may be that somebody else would be hurt in some way, or that something else is already around the corner that will look after our needs differently.

Witches can learn a lot about the nature of deep space by observing which of their unusual operations be successful, and which do not. The study of the Craft is thought about by most to be a long-lasting pursuit, with ongoing learning and refining of practices. When thinking about the relationship between the growth of the Universe and the development of the human brain, the wisdom of continuous study makes even more sense. As more knowing occurs, more magical techniques are developed and established, and there's all the more to capture upon.

Routine and Spellwork

It may be said that Wicca, as a religion, recognizes the laws of the Universe symbolically through the Goddess and God, the Wheel of the Year, and reverence for all living things.

Routines performed in celebration of these elements of deep space might or might not involve fantastic work, as some Wiccans prefer to

focus on what they see as the "spiritual" side of life. Witches, on the other hand, tend to blend routine with magic, and may focus solely on working to transform reality for the benefit of themselves and others. This does not always imply they don't consider themselves spiritual. If all matter includes all matter, then there is no separation between mental issues and the issues of everyday life.

Whether magic is being worked in a provided routine, Wiccans and other Witches tend to integrate a couple of common structures in their official activities, including casting a magical or sacred circle, conjuring up deities and special powers using unique words and phrases, and closing the loop at the end of the ritual. Motion, dance, shouting, or singing might likewise be part of the activities.

These formal actions communicate to the higher realms of deep space the thoughts and intents of the specialist(s) in a focused and productive manner, concentrating the energies of objective clearly and definitively. Voltage, as physical matter, is raised in ritual and directed towards specific purposes, whether for thankfulness and cvcnt, manifesting solutions to problems, or both.

Casting the Circle

As a symbol, the circle represents the Moon, the Earth, and the abundance of the Goddess. For this reason, a ring can safely contain the physical quantity of energy raised by the Witch or Witches carrying out the ritual, and see its transformation through to the higher realms. The circle is a considerably portable tool, as it can be drawn anywhere, either physically or psychically, subtly or elaborately, depending upon the scenarios.

The circle is small or as massive as suitable. However, it needs to have enough space for the altar, everything being used in the routine, and everybody getting involved-- I'll be introducing to you the platform and ritual tools in the next area. It is generally marked on the floor of the area being utilized for ritual, often with sea salt first, followed by candles, or other magical items charged with energy for ceremonies, such as crystals and semiprecious gemstones, and even herbs.

When energy is raised inside the circle, the circle should remain closed until the end of the ritual. This keeps the heat from joining distracting or unsuitable power from the rest of the real airplane, which reinforces the magic and protects professionals from unwanted energetic interference.

Nobody can step beyond the circle while it is active without first carrying out an energetic manipulation, such as a "circle-cutting" spell, which creates a dynamic "doorway" that is safe to reenter and exit. When the circle is re-entered, the door is closed, and the circle reconnected.

Calling the Quarters

Referred to as "drawing the quarters," this is a method of acknowledging the four primary directions and their Elemental associations, as well as the chosen divine beings of the coven or solitary Witch.

In a coven, either the High Priestess, the High Priest, or another coven member will walk the circle, stopping in each cardinal instructions to invoke the existence of its associated Element and, if suitable, god or goddess. (It must be remembered here that not all coven structures involve hierarchy-- some covens just have each member take turns performing this and any other necessary roles in ritual.) Specific words are typically spoken to invoke the special powers and true blessings of the component and deity being called. Once this is complete, the space is prepared for the heart of the routine.

Types of Ritual

The heart of the ritual may be a Sabbat or Esbat event, or it may celebrate a life occasion such as an initiation into a coven, a self-introduction for eclectic and singular Witches, a handfasting (wedding), or an end of life ceremony. There are as many variations on each of these types of routine as there are covens and solitary professionals, and the way a specific Sabbat or Esbat is commemorated may alter and change throughout the years. In truth, many routines are made up on the spot.

Moreover, the majority of covens don't share information about their rituals with non-members. All of this makes it challenging to generalize about the proceedings of routine in Witchcraft. Lots of examples are available in books about the Craft and on Other and Wiccan Pagan websites.

At some point during the ritual, fantastic spells may be worked. Prophecy may also be employed, particularly at Samhain, though this may take location after the ceremony. When all of the ritual work is finished, the circle is closed, frequently in an opposite way to the way it is opened, with the Witch thanking and dismissing the Elements and divine beings conjured up at the start, while strolling in the opposite instructions. This guarantees that the energy raised during ritual has gone entirely to its destination in the higher worlds, and is not squandered or ignored in the physical plane. It likewise assists ground the Witch(es) more firmly in the real airplane after reaching extreme states of awareness.

Magical Work

The types, forms, and intentions of fantastic work occurring during a Wiccan ritual are as differed as every other aspect of Wicca and Witchcraft: It may include any mix of actions, tools, words, complicated or easy spellwork, a tea or brew, chanting and motion, candlelight work, etc

. The choices for magical discovery are genuinely limitless. The function of the magic can also be anything under the sun-- as long as the effect is positive, and does no damage. Numerous Wiccans pick to work for spiritual in addition to material development, utilizing the Sabbats as opportunities to review their lives at each point in the Wheel and work for balance or any necessary change.

However, magical work does not need to become part of the Wiccan routine, and isn't limited to it. Witches will include incredible job, as they are likely and able to do so, into any part of their lives.

The tools described in the next area are utilized in both Wiccan routine and lots of other forms of Witchcraft, in the ways and for the functions that feel suitable to the Witch(es) who utilize them.

The Tools

Wiccans, as well as other Witches, incorporate a variety of items into their routines and magic, a number of which are familiar to traditional culture

-- you may have become aware of a few of these tools, and even have the ability to picture what they appear like, from viewing television and movies.

However, their discussion in the movie theater is frequently incorrect, with more emphasis put on entertainment rather than being depicting the reality of a tool's usage and purpose. For this reason, much of the Wiccan tools are misunderstood.

Given that the Universe is made of the idea, it is eventually the thought energy behind the actions performed with the tools that cause improvement of truth.

- **Broom**

Perhaps the most typical (and commonly misunderstood) sign of Witches and Witchcraft in popular culture, the broom has become part of Wiccan and other pagan lore around the world for centuries. The spiritual brush is not always used in the official Wiccan routine itself; however, it is typically utilized to sweep energetic clutter from the ritual area in advance. The bristles do not, in fact, have to touch the ground, as this sort of cleansing is taking place on the energetic and psychic level.

Because it functions as a cleanser, it is associated with the component of Water, and is spiritual to the Goddess. The broom can also be positioned near the entrance to a house to protect versus unfavorable or undesirable energy.

The broom can be any size, from miniature "decorative" brooms to bigger, full-sized brushes. It might even be a tree-branch utilized symbolically as a broom. Standard woods used for sacred brooms include birch, ash, and willow. Lots of Witches keep hand-made brushes for ritual functions. However, a typical home broom can also be devoted to the work of Witchcraft. No matter what type of product, nevertheless, the regular brush is never utilized for everyday housekeeping, as this would contaminate the sacred energy it holds for routine and magical purposes.

- **Altar**

The altar is the sacred location where tools are positioned during Wiccan ritual and magic. Generally, the platform stands in the center of the circle of energy raised by the participant(s) in the ceremony. It might be a table or other item with a flat surface, such as an old chest. It can be square or round, according to choice. Witches may embellish the altar with colored scarves or other products corresponding with the season or the particular function of the routine.

Ideally, the altar is made of wood, such as oak, which is considered to hold significant power, or willow, which is deemed to be spiritual to the goddess. It can actually be made of any product, as any real things charged with magical energy will contribute power to the routine work being enacted.

Witches performing outside routines might utilize an old tree stump, large stone, or other natural item for an altar, or may use a fire in place of the altar, putting the routine tools in other places in the charged space.

While the altar is usually set up prior to the ritual and taken down later, some Witches preserve long-term altars in their homes. These may function as shrines to the Goddess and God, and can be a place to keep the Witch's wonderful tools.

The tools are strategically positioned in specific styles on the altar, with deliberate regard to the components and the four instructions. For instance, tools and symbols related to the element of Earth may be placed in the North area of the altar, while those connected with water will be put to the East. Traditional Wiccan practice also typically devotes the left side of the altar to representations of the Goddess, while the ideal team represents the God. While numerous Witches carefully follow established patterns for setting up the platform, others will experiment and use designs that resonate with their relationship with their deities and matching tools and symbols.

- **Wand**

Used for millennia in magical and spiritual rites, the wand has long been connected with Witches and Witchcraft in popular culture, and has likewise been wholly misunderstood.

Similar to all wonderful tools, it is not the wand that causes magical transformation; however, the Witch, who energetically charges the rod with high intent. As a shape, it takes the type of a line; therefore, it is used to direct energy. It is typically used in Wiccan routine to conjure up the Goddess and God, and maybe utilized to draw magical signs in the air or on the ground. It may also be effectively used to illustrate the circle within which the ritual or spellwork is carried out. The wand is connected with the aspect of Air, and is considered spiritual to the God.

The wand can be a relatively straightforward affair, simply cut from a small branch or twig from a tree (with a mindset of respect and regard for the tree making the sacrifice). Generally, the wand isn't much longer than the forearm, and can be much shorter. Woods traditionally utilized to make the rod include oak, willow, senior, and hazel. Witches without access to these or other trees might buy a wood dowel from a craft or hardware shop to consecrate and embellish as a wand. There are also some exquisite glass or pewter-based rods embellished with engravings and crystals readily available at lots of New Age shops. Still, wood is the traditional product for Wiccan wands, and it is typically thought that a rod made by the Witch who uses it is more effective.

- **Knife**

Called an athame, the ritual knife, like the wand, is a tool that directs energy in ritual, and may likewise be utilized to draw the circle before ritual and close the loop afterward.

Nevertheless, it is more of an energy manipulator or commander, due to its sharp edges, and therefore isn't commonly used to invoke divine beings, as this would be considered robust, instead of collective, in regards to working with high energy. The athame is also utilized to draw beautiful symbols, such as the pentagram, in the air to lend power to routine and spellwork, and is frequently employed in methods that eradicate and launch negative energies or impacts. This tool is related to the God, and the component of Fire, as it is a representative that triggers modification.

The knife is typically sharp on both sides, with a black deal with which is stated to save a percentage of the radiant energy raised in routines for later use. The blade is not typically really long--the length of one's hand, or shorter, is thought about perfect.

Some Witches purchase special daggers to serve as their athame, while others will consecrate a regular cooking area knife for the purpose. It's thought about unwise to utilize a knife that has been used to cut animal flesh. However, any negative energies lingering from such usage can be ritually cleaned before "transforming" the blade into an athame. Some Witches choose to enhance their energetic relationship with their knife by inscribing excellent symbols into the deal with.

Depending on the custom, the athame may do double duty as a real cutting and engraving tool. It may be used to cut herbs, shape a brand-new wand from the branch of a tree, or carve magical symbols into a candle for routine usage. Nevertheless, many Witches prefer to use a second, white-handled knife (often called a boline) for these functions, keeping the athame for ritual usage just.

- **Cauldron**

While the word "cauldron" may evoke images of Shakespeare's three witches tossing all sorts of animal parts into a boiling stew for wicked functions, the cauldron is a sign of the Goddess and the innovative forces of change. Containers appear in several ancient Celtic myths in connection with magical incidents, and continue to influence Witchcraft today. Related to the aspect of Water, the cauldron might hold amazingly charged active ingredients for a potion, or might be utilized to permit spell candle lights to stress out. It can likewise be filled with freshwater and used for scrying.

Cast iron is considered the cauldron's perfect product, though other metals are typically used. A lot of rest on three legs, with the opening of the cauldron having a smaller diameter than the best part of the bowl. Cauldrons can vary from a few inches to a couple of feet across in size, though bigger sizes may be thought about not practical. While some Witches might brew an excellent potion right in the cauldron, the reasonable restraints of lighting a safe indoor fire below it tend to limit this use--often, the "brewing" aspect of the magic is symbolic rather than actual.

- **Cup**

Like the cauldron, the cup represents the aspect of Water and represents the fertility of the Goddess.

A crucial element of the altar layout during a routine, it might hold water, white wine, or potentially a unique tea brewed for the wonderful purpose of the rite. In some routines, it stays empty, as a symbol of preparedness to receive new sources of abundance from the Spirit world. Likewisecalled the "goblet" or the "chalice" in some traditions, it can be made of any quality compound such as earthenware, crystal, glass, or silver. Singular Witches may simply commit a favorite old household cup, charging it with magical energy and keeping it simple for this function.

- **Pentacle**

The pentacle is an important symbol-bearer in Witchcraft, usually inscribed with a pentagram, though other wonderful symbols might be available. The pentagram itself is a five-pointed star, drawn with five straight lines, typically encircled, and constantly having one upward point. Each point is said to represent the aspects of Air, Earth, Fire, and Water, with the Fifth Element (Spirit) as the upward point.

As a sign, it is discovered in both ancient Eastern and Western cultures and has been used to represent numerous elements of spiritual and human concerns. The pentagram is considered to have intrinsic magical powers, and is often inscribed on items in addition to in the air throughout rituals, to include strength to the work.

As a bearer of this Earth-related symbol, the pentacle is utilized to consecrate other tools and objects used in ritual. Typically a flat, round piece of wood, silver, wax, or clay, it can be any size, though typically is small enough to fit conveniently on the altar with the other tools. The pentacle might be ornately carved and set with semiprecious gemstones, or maybe an effortless style. Witches may also use a pentacle on a cable or chain throughout the ritual, and even as part of their daily gown, though they might or might pass by to wear it publicly.

- **Incense**

Incense is associated with the aspect of Air, and, in some customs, Fire. Smoldering incense is often positioned before images of the deities on an altar or a shrine. Many Witches feel that fragrance is a vital component of effective ritual. This is partly due to the consciousness-altering potential of quality incense, which can help with a more concentrated state of mind when performing magical work.

Smoke from the incense can likewise offer visions of the deities being conjured up in routine, or other images essential to the work being carried out. Particular herbs, spices, barks, and roots have specific magical qualities, so homemade incense blends can be utilized to strengthen magical spells.

Whether homemade or store-bought, regular Wiccan routines prefer granulated or raw incense, which needs charcoal briquettes to burn on, and is usually held in a censer. Some

Witches may let the scent smolder in the cauldron instead of a censer.

For Witches who are more sensitive to incense smoke, lighter stick or cone incenses may work better. Some go with scenting their magical candles with oils rather. Whatever the choice, it's typically agreed that some form of fragrant enhancement is optimal for magical work.

- **Crystals, Stones, Herbs, and Oils**

Possibly a few of the most effective magical tools are those that come straight from the Earth without much, if any, modification by human hands. Herbs and semiprecious gems have long been understood to have healing homes, and are used today in lots of medical systems around the globe. They are likewise utilized in Witchcraft, as decors, offerings, magical improvements, and even as the focus of some routines and spells.

Crystals and other stones have their energies and are considered to be "alive," instead of just dormant matter. Sensitive people can frequently feel their energies when holding these stones in their hands or on some other part of their bodies.

Some stones are used for specific functions in routine, while others might be more irreversible existences on the altar or in other places in a Witch's home. They might range in size from a square half-inch to much more significant, and maybe polished and sculpted into specific shapes, or left in their raw type. Crystals can be found in many New Age stores along with online, though they can, in some cases, still be found in their raw form in specific natural areas.

Crystals might be utilized to help defend against illness or negative energy, or may aid in divination or other psychic work. They might also be used to layout the magic circle at the start of the routine. These stones have astrological associations as well as associations with specific gods and goddesses.

Herbs are likewise associated with astrological bodies and specific deities, and are utilized in a variety of ways, consisting of excellent cooking area brews, edibles, and potions, and spell active ingredients. A few of the most common kitchen herbs, such as basil, thyme, and rosemary, also have magical associations, which doubles their capacity for practical magic, as they can be used to make "enchanted" foods.

Other herbs utilized in magic are not suitable to consume, and care needs always to be taken to understand the difference. It is considered ideal for Witches to collect their herbs with their routine knives, whether from a nearby woods or their own kitchen herb "gardens." However, fresh herbs can be discovered in grocery shops, and numerous natural food shops also sell a variety of dried herbs in their bulk departments.

Essential oils from nuts, seeds, and plants are used to boost routine environment and likewise as components in spellwork. Oils have esoteric properties and might be rubbed into spell candle lights for a particular excellent purpose, or used in a skin-safe blend to anoint the

body prior to the ritual. Witches often make their own blends of vital oils to strengthen routine and spellwork. Also used in aromatherapy for recovery a number of psychological and physical ailments, essential oils are commonly offered at health food stores.

- **Candle lights**

Last, however, certainly not least, candles are thought-about necessary to the practice of Witchcraft.

Candle lights have a magical way about them as they permit us to work straight with the component of fire. They serve as a source of light, as devotional signs of deity, as a way of communicating with Spirit, and to help change in many spells.

Witches deal with a range of candle light colors, depending on the deities being represented and/or invoked, in addition to any particular wonderful purposes of a routine or spell. Candles are a direct and basic way to deal with color magic. Colors have their own metaphysical properties, as well as astrological and elemental associations, which will be described in the next area of this guide.

Witches will usually identify in between candle lights used for particular routine functions and more "multi-purpose" candle lights utilized for additional lighting throughout spellwork (or merely to enhance any night atmosphere). Candle lights consecrated for wonderful use are therefore not used for any other purposes.

Other Tools

Depending upon the custom, the coven, and the specific Witch, additions and variations to the tools described above may be utilized in ritual and spellwork. For example, some Witches utilize a sword in addition to, or in a location of, the routine knife. Swords can be not practical for indoor routine due to their size, and are not as easily accessible as knives, and so are less typically utilized.

A staff is likewise often used in formal routine, held by the High Priest or Priestess of a coven. Like the wand, it brings the representations of Air and the God, though, in some customs, it represents Fire. It is typically made of wood and might be decorated with wonderful signs and semiprecious stones.

Lots of Witches also incorporate prophecy tools in their ritual practice. These may consist of runes, tarot cards, a quartz crystal sphere (or "crystal ball") for scrying or other oracles borrowed from older customs, such as the I-Ching. Specific items, such as a particular Tarot card or rune, might be included in spells for particular purposes. The crystal sphere is typically utilized on the altar to represent the Goddess. As mentioned previously, divination might occur during an official routine, however, post-ritual is likewise considered an excellent time for this activity, as the Witch is still in a conducive state of mind to communicate with the Spirit world at this time.

Lastly, lots of Witches like to consist of amazingly charged jewelry and other aspects of "outfit" into their practice. Some may simply wear a pentacle on a chain, as pointed out above, while others may put on unique robes and a headpiece encrusted with gemstones to enhance their energy throughout the ritual. Witches in some customs likewise work naked, which is typically referred to as "sky-clad.".

Just like any other element of Wicca and Witchcraft, there is no set-in-stone way to approach utilizing the tools of routine and magic. While it's generally considered handy to use at least a couple of, if not numerous, of the mechanisms described above, it is ultimately about the Witch and his or her connection to the specific tools selected, or the coven members' cumulative affinities for the specifics of their ritual practice. Those recognizing as Wiccans are likely to have some symbolic representation of the Goddess and God at Sabbat celebrations, and the Goddess at Esbats, but the method this is performed can differ extensively.

While some solitaries and covens may develop intricate routines utilizing every tool imaginable, others may develop extremely basic affairs, including just a crystal and candlelight. In other words, it's more about using what feels inspiring and "in tune," rather than collecting items from a checklist-- if it feels out of location, or unpleasantly unusual to a particular Witch to buy and utilize a cauldron or a censer, or wear unique robes, then these items might simply not be essential or suitable for that person.

This is, naturally, a really brief introduction of the basic concepts, tools, and forms associated with Wicca and other Witchcraft, as opposed to a thorough conversation-- as is to be expected with such a different and commonly varying faith as Wicca, other sources will have different things to say about a number of the subjects talked about here. Readers interested in discovering more ought to seek advice from as many referrals as they please for a much deeper understanding of these beliefs and practices.

For those considering adopting any or all of the practices talked about in this guide, the next area will explore numerous practical steps one can take on their journey towards practicing Wicca.

CHAPTER THIRTEEN

Tips For Aspiring Wiccans

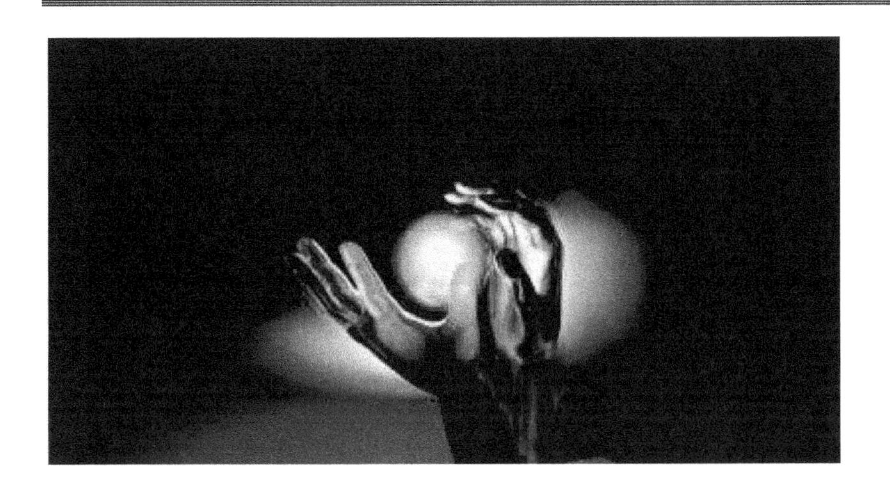

- **Moving Forward**

Wicca is different from other religious beliefs in many aspects. It doesn't tend to be evangelistic or look for new members; you won't discover numerous fliers welcoming you to the next Sabbat celebration with your local coven.

This leaves it to the individuals intrigued in the Craft to look for info and possible connections with others in the Wiccan community. Luckily, the Internet has made it far much more comfortable than it used to be for Witches and Wiccans to post and find info and interact with each other.

- **Read And Check Out**

The very best way to start is to read widely about Wicca and other kinds of Paganism. If you read commonly enough, you'll come across conflicting beliefs and recommendations, and this is an excellent thing, as it enables you to establish your understanding of the forces and phenomena at work in Wicca and Witchcraft. Follow what resonates with you at the deepest level. If a ritual, spell, any other idea, or a particular viewpoint does not attract you, leave it out of your establishing practice and keep seeking more information that feels "ideal." A lot of Wiccans and Witches will inform you that it takes a long period to study and observe to produce an authentic individual relationship with the Craft.

If you're looking to link with others, depending upon where you live, there may be a local coven, circle, or other such groups that you could join or find a way out for information and recommendations. You can likewise examine event listings online, in regional newspapers, or other neighborhood resources. You can send out an intent to the Universe to assist in bringing the people you're looking for into your life, and it may be that a group near you is looking for somebody new to sign up with and will look forward to receiving your message!

You can also always begin your own "study group" to discover like-minded souls who also wish to find out more about Wicca, Witchcraft, or other forms of Paganism.

- **Coven, Circle, Solitary, Or Eclectic?**

For people interested in working with other Wiccans and Covens, circles and witches can be a great way to get more robust training and advice from experienced practitioners. The terms "coven" and "circle" can be confusing for newbies, as they typically appear to be used interchangeably. They are not, nevertheless, the same thing.

A circle is generally a relatively informal group whose members may get together to find out and talk about the Craft and might try out the different types of routine and spellwork. They might or might not fulfill for Sabbats and Esbats, depending on the collective wishes of the group. Depending upon how "open" the group is, there might be numerous members, some of whom drop in and out as it matches them, or simply a few routinely included good friends. The structure of a circle is typically loose and does not need official initiation or involves an established hierarchy.

A coven, on the other hand, is more structured and typically has several established leaders, such as a High Priestess or High Priest, particularly in what is described as "Traditional" Wicca. Covens meet for Esbats and Sabbats, and members are anticipated to go to these gatherings, as the involvement of everyone is necessary to the routine. Initiation is usually needed, though it's somewhat not likely that somebody brand-new to Wicca will be rapidly initiated into a coven, for a few factors.

One is that covens are generally small groups, with seven being considered an ideal number, and there's a custom of not more than 13 members, if there's sufficient reason to push a coven past 13, one member will depart to start a new, separate coven. Depending on how well established a coven is, there might just merely not be any openings.

Secondly, coven members will want potential brand-new initiates to have spent a good deal of time studying before considering inviting them to take part in the official routine.

Finally, given that the bonds formed between coven members are relatively intimate and strong, the concern of whether somebody's personality and general energy are a good fit is an important one.

For those who do not live near any circles or covens, or who just prefer not to include a social aspect into their experience of the Craft, the life of a diverse or singular Witch can be simply as significant and fulfilling. Perhaps you 'd rather be familiar with the magical and spiritual dimensions of the Universe on your own for a while, and then consider connecting to like-minded others, or maybe you're just born to be a solo specialist, who's completely fine! No matter which instructions you pick, there's a myriad of scholarly sources out there to guide you along the way.

The terms "solitary" and "eclectic" may often be used interchangeably, as there can be a great deal of overlap, but the differences deserve explaining here. " Solitary" refers to the practice of Wicca or Witchcraft on one's own, without any group experience such as a coven or circle. Wiccans who come from covens may (and frequently do) still practice by themselves, along with their involvement in coven work. However, a Solitary Wiccan or Witch always works alone. A singular Witch can even intentionally follow what is typically accepted be "Traditional" Wicca, such as Gardnerian, British Traditional Wicca, or another "lineage-based" tradition, and those who do so tend to determine as "singular" rather than "diverse.".

" Eclectic" is a description for Witches who do not follow a single, particular tradition and instead borrow and blend concepts, techniques, practices, etc. from a range of sources, and might also (and typically do) invent their own. Some covens likewise consider themselves to be "eclectic," although this tends to irritate members of traditional covens.

It's worth remembering here that even the earliest recognized kinds of Traditional Wicca were primarily obtained, mixed, and " invented" themselves.

Finding Your Way In.

In this area, I want to show you how a newcomer to Wicca may begin to embrace the Wiccan beliefs, way of living, and rituals.

- **Living through the Wheel of the Year.**

Wicca and Witchcraft are rooted in a relationship with nature and its different expressions in plant and animal life, the aspects, and the turning of the seasons. The living, breathing Divine Mind is vibrantly present in nature, maybe more certainly so than in many of the human-made, modern-day, "industrialized world." Those interested in Wicca and Witchcraft will benefit from consciously observing the natural world around them and establishing a more deliberate relationship with it.

Witches who live in climates with four different seasons (Spring, Summer, Autumn, and Winter) have an exceptional opportunity to observe the Wheel of the Year carefully. Sabbats are the very best time to keep in mind the modifications on the Earth and in the sky over the last several weeks, and Esbats also provide celebrations for marking the seasons' effects in our everyday lives. The more you take note of the area "in-between seasons," the more the motion of the Earth ends up being obvious even in Winter.

If you live in an environment with less seasonal range, or even none at all to speak of, you can still observe the effects of natural forces in subtle methods. The sun still casts various qualities of light throughout the day. The air tends to change simply before the rain. Ending up being practiced in the practice of observing little details in your natural surroundings helps cultivate your openness to the hidden energies inherent in all of the Universe.

If you can, go out for walks, hikes, picnics, etc. in places with soil and vegetation. Or go swimming, canoeing, or rock-skipping throughout a pond. Construct a snowman or shape your creation in snow. Do whatever you can to invest some quality time outdoors regularly.

If you reside in an urban environment and have little in the way of access to natural areas, you can still produce ways to interact with the hidden forces of deep space. Parks can be ideal, however, so can indoor plants and windowsill gardens. You can grow herbs for magical use and recovery, along with cooking. Open a window at dawn and study whatever you can see of the sky. Stand in the rain for a minute and accept the sensation of it on your skin. Even nature programs and photos or art portraying natural scenes can help put you in touch, along with recordings of nature sounds and meditation music.

When Sabbats come around, make a point of gathering a few of the seasonal presents of the Earth-- flower petals in Spring months leaves shed from deciduous trees in Autumn, pine needles from evergreens in Winter. Use these in routine, or just as designs on your cooking area table or elsewhere where you'll see them typically. As you practice these ways of observing the Wheel of the Year, you'll find your relationship with the seasons (even your least preferred ones) becoming more attuned and rooted in appreciation.

- **Deities And The Divine.**

Seeking and attaining a spiritual relationship with the Triple Goddess or Cernunnos or Diana or any other number of divine beings from around the ancient world can be an extremely effective method into the Craft, and lots of people find their experience to be deepened and sharpened through the practice of more standard, structured types of Wicca.

Some beginners to Wicca and Witchcraft are not sure about the concept of "worshipping" deities, and may feel odd about browsing for one or more specific gods or goddesses to form relationships or alignments with. Loaning from older customs in this regard might not quite seem like an authentic method to a spiritual search.

It indeed takes time to discover and cultivate an interest in and a relationship with a deity you weren't familiar with until just recently, and individuals who were raised in monotheistic religious beliefs can have a hard time even more with integrating the idea of polytheism. It's likewise real that you don't have to incorporate a faith in or a relationship with any particular form of the divine. You may just deal with the concept of a Goddess and a God, and even less definitively recognized energies of the Universe.

Faith and belief are far more frequently established and cultivated gradually than right away achieved. Make an effort to study and seek yours, however, go at your rate, and trust your intuition. Because your relationship with the divine doesn't match their experience, no one can inform you you're not a real Wiccan or Witch. (Well, some might, however, in religion with numerous variations, it's just natural that some will quibble about the details.) There's no intermediary in between you and deep space, and there are as numerous paths to the Divine as there are individuals who seek it.

If you do see getting in touch with deities as a possible part of your path, begin doing some research study. Check them out in Wiccan books, in ancient misconceptions, in poetry, in history books. You may find, as some Witches do, that a deity will discover you through images, dreams, relatively "random" coincidences or events, or in other ways.

- **Meditation and Visualization.**

Getting ready for ritual and magical work includes accessing an advantageous altered state of mind that permits both openness and focus. Lots of traditions practice particular meditation and visualization techniques to enhance this ability and call on it when required. You can find information on meditation in Witchcraft or lots of other spiritual customs. Seek out various kinds of meditation instruction and practice what works best for you. If absolutely nothing else, be sure to set aside time and space for privacy and reflection, preferably every day, however absolutely before routine and spellwork.

A Ritual of Celebration and Magic Adopted for the Autumn Equinox.

This reasonably simple ritual is provided as one example of many possibilities-- I've included it to reveal you an example of one of the more accessible, and easy-to-perform routines for the novice Wiccan. It's created for solitary practice but could be adapted for use with a coven. Like the majority of routines, it can be tailored to your intuition, choices, or circumstances. (It can likewise be duplicated for other Sabbats, with modifications made to seasonal products, candle colors, etc.) You need to have a candle or two at least, and some kind of recognition of the season to serve as points of focus for your energy remember, most of the tools are symbolic as the power comes from you.

However, tools are especially useful for beginners as they provide them something tangible to focus and direct their energy onto.

Are you prepared to begin?

Given That the Autumn Equinox is a time for commemorating the abundance of the harvest, styles for focus in ritual consist of appreciation to the Sun for making the harvest possible and to the Earth for yielding plenty to finish the Winter months.

The balance of equivalent day and equivalent night is likewise excellent to observe, as is the opportunity to begin a turning inward and eagerly anticipating a more relaxing time. When the abundance of the Earth starts to die back to make room for brand-new development in the next cycle, the end of Summer is also a time. We can use this time to recognize what in our lives isn't required any longer, whether it be excessive "things," an old habit we've wished to break, or anything else that we 'd like to release back into deep space.

As you prepare for the routine, practice meditation on these styles and observe what comes to mind. See this opportunity to gain insight into an element of your life; you might not have been conscious of previously.

Advised items:

- Seasonal representations such as late summer season crops, mainly corn and squash, marigolds, seeds, and apples.
- Candle lights: 1 black, one white, one dark green spell candle, and one or more others in fall colors like red, orange, brown, gold, etc.
- Pentacle Cup Incense or oils: frankincense, sandalwood, pine, rosemary, chamomile Stones: jade, carnelian, lapis lazuli Herbs: sage, Hawthorne, cedar Instructions: Layout your tools on your altar or ritual space.

One way is to position the white candlelight on the left for the Goddess, the black candle on the right for the God, the pentacle to the North, and the cup to the West. Candlelight can be positioned in the South, this can be the spell of candlelight, if you're using it. Incense or oils can be put in the East. (If it's not useful to position burning incense right on the altar, you can position it somewhere close by in the Eastern quarter.) Any stones or representations of the harvest can be placed around the edges of the altar or wherever they seem to "want" to be. Take some time trying various arrangements. You'll soon get a sense of what feels and looks right for you.

If you wish to cast a circle, ensure you have everything you're using for the routine, and then decide how big your ring will require to be. Using sea salt, sprayed candle lights, stones, or herbs, mark out the circle on the ground. Charge the loop with an intention for developing a spiritual space by slowly walking clockwise around it from the inside. As you stroll, "draw" the circle once again by pointing with your index finger, envisioning the energetic connection in between your body and the circle's edge, keep in mind, you are developing a place of higher, more powerful energy than will exist on the outside of the circle. This is an act that requires learning and consistent practice. It is not strictly necessary. However, it is a time-honored part of the Wiccan tradition that numerous discover to be important.

Light the white and black candles and invite the God and Goddess (or the balanced forces of male and woman) to be present with you in the celebration. If you wish, call the quarters by turning to stand in each primary instructions, starting with North and moving clockwise. Verbally acknowledge each direction by name and its associated aspect, and request its energy to come into your circle. You are already incorporating signs of the Elements with the pentacle (Earth), the incense or oil (Air), the candles (Fire), and the cup (Water) so you might hold each of these items as you welcome the Elements, either instead of calling the quarters or as part of it.

Show on the abundance you've experienced in the past season. Identify seven things you are grateful for and state them aloud. These can be little things or bigger ones-- whatever you feel genuinely thankful for at this time. Ask for any aid you need with developing balance, keeping security, and letting go of something.

If you're using a spell candlelight, rub a drop or 2 of essential oil into it, or simply hold it in your hands for a couple of moments. Visualize yourself feeling safe and grateful for the abundance in your life, in excellent physical health, and emotionally balanced. Out loud, state this vision in whatever method appears most natural to you. You may just say, "I have whatever I require. I am in health. My life is balanced." Light the green candle as you say the words. Then "seal" the deal with the last expression. Many Witches use the following: "So let it be," "So mote it be," "Blessed Be," or "It is done." Whatever you select, make sure to knowingly launch your objectives into the higher worlds where they can be changed and manifest. Enjoy the flame for a few moments, feeling the favorable energies raised within you and all around you in the sacred area.

When you're ready, thank the Elements, then the Goddess and God for their existence. Close the circle by strolling around it counter-clockwise, releasing its energy into the Universe. (Note: Don't leave any candles ignored, but do let the spell candle stress out on its own, if at all possible.).

Over the next couple of weeks, continue the practice of recognizing abundance and revealing thankfulness. You might likewise observe any seeming imbalances in your life or wellness and choose to do what you can to remedy them. If you do so, you will see that deep space will support you!

What Does Manifestation Look Like?

When Witches speak of "symptom" or "success" concerning prayer, intention, or spellwork, what do they imply? You do not tend to hear fairytale-like stories about vast, overnight gains in one's lifestyle the day after working a spell, though anything can take place if all the best situations remain in place. What innovative professionals of the Craft understand is that practice is needed in the form of research study, time, and experiment. One likewise has to cultivate a mindset that is open to manifestation, to success, and positive and wonderful incidents.

This can be a hard routine to obtain and hold onto, and everybody has their blind spots now and once again, however with active practice, the wonders of deep space begin to unfold more progressively.

Let me show you how.

When upon a time, a young, aiming Witch met an older, far more skilled Witch at a folk festival, where they were both outdoor camping in the woods. As the celebration wound down and everyone was evacuating to leave, the two Witches decided to exchange their contact info. Neither had a writing implement, nor could they discover any in their tents or packs. Then suddenly, the more youthful Witch spotted a pencil, "randomly" resting on the forest flooring in between 2 trees. "Wow," said the older Witch. "Talk about manifesting!".

The more youthful Witch was confused. How was this an example of "manifesting"? The pencil hadn't fallen from the sky, or perhaps been suddenly provided by a passerby out of the blue. Sure, it was a welcome coincidence, however clearly some other individual had simply lost a pencil in that spot in the woods, and over a celebration weekend, those woods saw their fair share of human artifacts. Besides, no spell or necromancy had been performed. So how did this pencil count as a symptom?

The more youthful Witch was too accustomed to analyzing the possible causes of occasions to appreciate the synchronicity and Divine timing of this pencil's development into her reality. Instead of focusing on the inherent magic of this small event, she instinctively transferred to dismiss it in favor of the regular "logical" thinking instilled in her through cultural conditioning.

This is a difficulty faced by numerous who are brand-new to the Craft, however, with consistent determination to be available to the subtleties of truth below our "reasonable" experience, it ends up being much easier to recognize all type of manifestations, from the "little things" to much larger improvements in our lives.

There are a few essential components in this specific event that satisfy the conceptual requirements of symptoms. The pencil appeared in the ideal location at the best time. Second, it fulfilled a particular need that, if met, would be useful to both individuals included, and would harm no one. Third, it happened in such a way that was unforeseen, instead of as an outcome of searching in all the apparent, rational locations for something to compose with. Symptom typically comes in methods we might never have thought of or prepared for, and as an extra-nice touch, it took place in a natural setting: a forest of old, splendid trees.

Only as significantly, the pencil was acknowledged as a symptom by the older Witch, who understood from practice how to recognize and value it as such. She also realized that symptoms could happen with or without designated spellwork. Often deep space merely assists in minutes of requirement or crisis-- these occasions are sometimes called "wonders." Since the older Witch was well-grounded in magical principles, she was frequently able to plan for things right away and did so regularly, always growing in her capability to connect her power with the Divine.

Beyond routine, intention-setting, and spellwork, the practice of taking notes and acknowledging with appreciation is just as crucial to affective symptoms. As you start seeing synchronicities in your life, nevertheless small, take note and remember them. You may wish to tape incidents that appear considerable in a journal or Book of Shadows. You will discover that the more you take note of them, the more you will draw in positive symptoms in your life.

- **Keeping a Book of Shadows.**

The term "Book of Shadows" comes out of the Gardnerian Tradition, however, has been widely embraced and adjusted by eclectics, covens, and solitaries ever considering that. Keeping one is an excellent way for skilled and brand-new Witches alike to deepen their practice of the Craft.

You can consider your Book of Shadows as a sort of journal, particularly for wonderful and/or spiritual pursuits. The contents of a Book of Shadows are individual and will differ from Witch to Witch. Some keep detailed directions for rituals and spells, either borrowed from other sources or of their own innovation. Some diligently record the results of their magical workings, information about their individual deity alignments, or lists of specific herbs and stones they feel an affinity with. Others might free-write about their intentions for a certain routine or a brand-new season. This can likewise be a good location to tape-record relevant dreams or other signs and messages that enter into your life. It's often illuminating to revisit these at a later date and see underlying connections between apparently unassociated phenomena!

These are just a couple of tips for digging deeper into the world of Wicca and Witchcraft. As we've seen, it's a highly varied and broad faith with many possible opportunities to follow. No matter what you do, always follow your instinct when it comes to how, when, and if you want to start the course of the Craft.

CONCLUSION

Unlike the majority of other Western faiths, Wicca is extremely decentralized, there is no official sacred text, no main governing body, and this means there is nobody way to practice the religion.

With this in mind, it is extremely tough to create a novice's guide on this topic, simply because different Wiccans will interpret the various facets of the belive in a different way.

In this guide, I have actually attempted to provide an impartial technique, though unquestionably, my own experiences as a practicing Wiccan may have influenced certain areas of this book. Generally speaking, I have actually tried to cover the most "popular" technique in each chapter above, as this will make the information much easier to absorb, and you are likewise most likely to meet Wiccans with the very same set of beliefs that truly resonate with you.

There is no right or wrong. As long as you keep the Wiccan principles at heart, and never ever intentionally seek to damage others, you can practice Wicca in any way you see fit. I would actively encourage you to look for your own path. One of the very best things about Wicca is that your beliefs, interpretations, and views are extremely versatile. When you are just starting out, you are encouraged to check out and discover as much as possible, and so your initial beliefs are bound to be shaped by the guides you check out.

Over time, when you begin to embrace Wicca in your day-to-day life, you might have special surprises that re-shape your method of practicing this faith. What you think on day one might be extremely different from your beliefs on day 100, which could be a world apart from your views on day 1,000. It can be a lifelong journey, and even after years, you will still discover yourself finding out new things.

Remember: nobody can inform you how to practice Wicca, and the religion can indicate anything you want it to suggest to you. While I have provided the info in this guide as "appropriate," I remain in no chance implying that it is the only way to practice Wicca. If you check out other guides, there might be clashing details. And when you checked out another guide to the subject, you will likely encounter much more contrasting info!

I will leave you with that thought, as it is now time for you to begin your journey, and interpret the info presented to you in your way. I sincerely hoped you delighted in finding out about Wicca with me, as it is a subject close to my heart. It would suggest a good deal to me if you continue on your path towards Wicca, however, if you choose not to, I hope I have educated you on the belief system of the terrific people who pick to practice Wicca.

WICCA BOOK OF SPELLS

A Guide to Candle Magic, Herbal Spells, Crystal, Witchcraft and Wiccan Belief

Karen Spells

Disclaimer

All erudition supplied in this book is specified for educational and academic purposes only. The author is not in any way to be responsible for any outcomes that emerge from using this book. Constructive efforts have been made to render information that is both precise and effective. Still, the author is not to be held answerable for the accuracy or use/misuse of this information.

Foreword

I will like to thank you for taking the very first step of trusting me and deciding to purchase/read this life-transforming book. Thanks for investing your time and resources on this product.

I can assure you of precise outcomes if you will diligently follow the specific blueprint I lay bare in the information handbook you are currently checking out. It has transformed lives, and I firmly believe it will equally change your own life too.

All the information I provided in this Do It Yourself piece is easy to absorb and practice.

INTRODUCTION

This book includes all the details needed for you to grip an understanding of the basics of the Wiccan believe and to discover how to harness the power of nature and to command it to produce the outcomes you desire. As you will know, Witchcraft is a holistic custom that includes all elements of the spiritual and natural world.

Much of the contents are non-denominational and can be practiced by any person of any faith. Consider this book as your initial step towards an understanding of the Craft and make sure you are open-minded to recognize the charm of the Craft and to accept the change it can bring to your life.

CHAPTER ONE

Gainingan Understanding of theCraft

Without a clear understanding and clear definitions of the terms Wicca, you can not easily find your foot to start learning the practices of Witchcraft, magick, and Paganism. Here we begin by explaining the distinctions amongst all these terms to assist you in constructing a foundation of understanding on which to build on as you check out the whole book.

Paganism

Paganism is an umbrella term for several religious beliefs. The term comprisessomespiritual beliefs; it was a term used to describe people who thought in a variety of gods, goddesses, or divine beings. Generally, paganism represents the pre-Christian religions that have come from several ancient traditions.

The Differences between Wicca and witchcraft

The terms 'Wicca' and 'Witchcraft' are often used interchangeably, but there are significant differences between the two.

Wicca

Wicca is a religion, nature-driven, an earth-centered religion. It, therefore, consists of praise of and observance to divine beings and spirits and is related to as a subset of Paganism. Wiccan Rede is the 'one Law' concept of Wicca that can be summed up as 'harm none.'

Witchcraft

Even in the absence belief system centered on spirituality, goddesses, or gods, one can use herbs and spells for protection, love, recovery, and so on, which suggests that even atheists might practice Witchcraft. Because of this, one may be a believer in any religion or none; but still, has the ability to practice Witchcraft as an art of using energy and the power in nature for an end goal. Lots of nations and cultures have their techniques in Witchcraft, and the term much includes there.

Practicing Wicca and Witchcraft.

Witchcraft may be practiced to heal or to destroy. Numerous forms of Witchcraft entail love, recovery, and protection using herbs, minerals, alternative science, and harnessing of energy to perform. Witchcraft is as diverse as lots of cultures of peoples throughout the world and can be high or adverse as the person acting it. The word used to define a person practicing either healing or hurting magick is called 'Witch.'

Thus, there is a difference in intent between Wicca and Witchcraft. Wicca's intent is positioning with the divine and a spiritual journey. At the same time, Witchcraft does not have to consist of spirituality or the divine in any form since spells might be cast, and meditation might be practiced, or herbs used even without calling upon any high spirits or deities. It is easy just to practice Witchcraft without any background in Wicca.

Because of the centuries in history involving the persecution of Witches by Christianity, there is a stigma connected to the title of being a 'witch,' and the word ended up being more of an allegation instead of an accepted title. During such challenging times, those practicing witchcraft wouldn't even recognize themselves as witches or scared of their security, while there is the freedom to determine as a Witch today, the negative undertones that still hover around the word hinder its appropriate use and obscure its real meaning. Many people are very first introduced to the idea of Witchcraft or Wicca through Hollywood movies, and the analysis is a twisted one, not offering the entire accurate picture of the concepts. Witches and Wiccans are both alike in the battles and obstacles they face in their neighborhoods, where they are shunned and even actively battled against for practicing.

Magick

There are several reasons for individuals being drawn towards magic. Some wish to comprehend their place in this vast universe; some are looking for responses to the different questions they have about life and almost everything around it, some others are seeking a life of magic and increased fact, which can be referred to as a life of marvel and mystery.

Let us initially go over why we often discover the term 'magic" and how it is different from the term 'magick.' 'Magick' is a term created by Aleister Crowley, founder of a Pagan religion called Thelema. He used the alternative spelling to distinguish the magic of the occult from that carried out on stages for entertainment. Other spellings have been embraced over time, such as " magick," "Majik," and "magic", but for no specific reason. Hence the term' magick' is mostly unnecessary, and all types are interchangeable, but we have embraced his concept in this book just by preference.

Magick can be loosely explained as the adjustment of the physical world via metaphysics by using ritual action.

Prayers are not viewed as magick; they are demands for magnificent intervention. When the names of Gods or divine beings are used in magick, it can end up being confusing, but it is essential to recognize whether the name is used as a demand or as a word of power.

An Introduction to Charms and spells

Of course, Witchcraft wouldn't be witchcraft without appeals and spells! The emotional drive is a significant source of power when casting spells and charms. It is essential you feel a strong passion for your periods to work, so it becomes a magick to you when it works perfectly.

It is not essential to be a fan of the Wiccan faith to cast spells and appeals. Any person can find out to appropriate way to throw a Circle and work a period of charm efficiently, no matter what their religious beliefs are, if any.

CHAPTER TWO

TheFundamentalsOf TheCraft

The Craft: Beliefs & Worship

All religious beliefs acknowledge a genderless force, a higher power beyond human understanding that we want to interact with to fulfill the request of our inner desires. Each religion has established its own natural life-ruling supreme authority to which they direct their worship.

Considering that Wicca is a religion that is mostly based upon nature, it is only sensible then that the Wiccan deities belong to both feminine and masculine kinds, as all in life manifests itself from this duality. Hence the 'Ultimate Deity' is divided into God and Goddess. Various denominations of Wicca stemming from different traditions have differing names for their divine beings and varying types.

A deity's name is merely a label, what is most important is what the deity represents and the qualities that you are worshipping. You may be sure that the God or Goddess you are praying or worshipping will not be confused as to whom you are resolving!

The Idea of Reincarnation

The belief is quite old and forms a part of diverse religious beliefs, for example, Buddhism and Hinduism. The theory asserts that this soul, spirit, or magnificent fragment is required to undergo all life experiences for the functions of its development. For example, having a look at Mozart, the belief that, at five years old, he likely maintained knowledge from his previous lifetime, allowing him to write concertos of genius type effectively, is a reasonable explanation for the phenomenon that would otherwise make little sense.

Reincarnation may be stretched to numerous examples; let's look at a homosexuality being. Sensations and sexual feelings from a previous life may roll over to the next, describing why some people have tendencies that are thought about 'abnormal' by scientific analyses.

In Wicca practice, it is a belief that not only humans have souls, but all things. Some religions believe there is an idea of rebirth in different ways, a human in this life, an animal, or a plant in the next life.

To describe the truth that the population is growing, Wicca acknowledges that there are also births of new souls, and therefore existing in us are either 'old' souls, which have been reincarnated and experienced several lives or 'brand-new' souls, which are starting their journey of experience.

Three Fold Retribution

An idea intimately linked to reincarnation is the idea of retribution or 'Karmic action.' Karmic action is considered a system that spans throughout the lifetime of a soul, in which any evil done by you in one lifetime will come at the expense through punishment in the next lifetime.

Wiccan beliefs, retribution takes place, not across several lifetimes, but within the same lifetime, which implies that Wiccan belief your benefit or penalty for the way you have lived your life is not gotten after death, instead, throughout your lifetime as you live it. Where things get even more fascinating in Wicca is that the Wiccan belief system is based on not only retribution for actions, however three-fold retribution, A three-fold retaliation means that for every good you do, you will have the opportunity of being rewarded three times as much. On the other hand, for any evil you do, you are punished three times as much. Naturally, it is not actual, but the principle is such.

The Wiccan system of belief then asserts that the experiences of a previous lifetime do not determine a life time's experience, and there may or might not be resemblances between the experiences throughout your present lifetime.

CHAPTER THREE

Channeling Your Focus

Every individual has what is known as 'psychic abilities,' that is, a capability beyond physical ability, of higher consciousness. While mental capacity may be apparent in some, it does not indicate those who don't show these abilities don't possess it; it merely shows that it is inactive.

For example, you would need to evaluate it by exerting your strength in different methods, and by carrying out various tasks according to your psychic ability. To discover your psychic abilities, you have to check it and carry out different tasks.

Channeling is a way of taking advantage of your higher awareness, allowing you to get otherwise unattainable information.

Mental Channelingand Physical Channeling

There are two significant categories channeling ability falls under. These two categories are Mental and Physical.

Physical Channeling-- this relates to an impact on material objects. Activities including radiesthesia (the pendulum), cartomancy (card reading), tasseography (tea-leaf reading) and psychometry, are physical channeling activities.

Psychological Channeling-- this associate with impressions that are gotten in conscious awareness, at some level. This classification covers activities like clairsentience (sensing), clairvoyance (clear seeing), clairaudience (hearing), and telepathy (idea transfer). Also included herein are retrocognitive and precognitive functions in the present time.

Trance Channeling& Conscious Channeling

There are likewise two types of channeling that exist. These types are 'trance' channeling and conscious channeling. Within the category of trance' channeling, there are deep, medium, and light states of trance. If a channeler happens to be in a daze, the conscious mind is not engaged throughout the channeling process, and the channeler will not recall any details or know what they are seeing or saying throughout the time they are transporting.

In conscious channeling, however, as it suggests, the conscious mind actively takes part in the channeling. This indicates that the brain is analyzing the data that the higher conscious receives, it examines and gets involved by facial expression, body language, and voice inflection.

Ending up being a Channel

To harness your channeling capabilities and begin channeling, it is needed first to eliminate all challenges in mind. Your mind is occupied with accumulated problems, things like inhibitions, indecision, uncertainty, criticism, and incorrect values and all sorts of things that have developed and settled over your lifetime. These things hamper the circulation of energy and info in your mind, tying up our psychic capability.

The Focus of the Conscious Mind

Mind Control

To begin putting things in order right in your mind and to communicate with your higher awareness, it is vital to learn the art of focusing and controlling your account. That is an indication that you require to start targeting if you have numerous ideas running through your mind at once. Spread ideas result in spread energy, which implies that when you believe you are focusing on something, you are, in fact, just giving it a small part of your strength. Controlling mental energy enables you to use your undistracted attention on something, offering you power. This power can be compared to a force of production, which you can use to bring your magic to life.

Elimination of Emotions

It is essential to attain the complete elimination of these toxic emotions to get real spiritual quality. Unlimited love offers no space for envy, hate anger, or greed.

Continuous Self-Examination

When seeking truth, it is needed to undergo consistent self-assessment. It is very to determine what your beliefs and ideas are and to attain concise morals for yourself. Develop your objectives, define them plainly, and identify specific items to work towards. Afterward, it is needed that you prioritize your goals and pursue them in the order you have attentively put them in.

Getting rid of Materialism

Things and people tend to rule over your affairs, acting as though they are servants. These things take money and time, tying you down and complicating your life.

Learn Genuine Love

Learning how to love genuinely is essential, and many misconceptions are surrounding this idea. Love itself is sometimes mistaken as self-centered, or lustful. A greater love does exist, one which is unselfish and has to do with the release, instead of the attachment. Love has to do with understanding and forgiving. It is necessary to acknowledge that every individual has their course to follow and lessons to discover to walk their journey at their speed.

Learn the Art of Meditation

The art of meditation is best understood as a process through which you can listen to your higher self. Meditation assists with concentration and with focussing attention on the higher level of awareness that is present in every one of us. A daily period of reflection can clear the mind of clutter and preserve a clear channel of communication.

CHAPTER FOUR

The Basics Of Meditation

Meditation can best be described as 'listening.' When appropriately used, meditation leads to individual improvement. Meditation is the most basic of all the techniques of spiritual growth, and it may be practiced in a group or even alone.

Meditation is a practice that quietens our conscious mind, the mind which is interested in everyday activities and life as you understand it. It enables you to transmit your higher consciousness, also regarded as subconsciousness, the part of your mind that is accountable for uncontrolled physical functions, reflex actions, and what you might call 'Universal Memory.'

The Dynamics of Meditation

To understand the dynamics of meditation, initially, the make-up of the human consciousness needs to be recognized, and it also needs to be acknowledged that people are both spiritual and physical beings. These two elements of humanity are connected at the interpretive centers, which are described by their Sanskrit descriptions-- Chakras. Throughout the act of meditation, psychic energy travels through these chakras. The kundalini force is a potent force referred to as the 'Serpent Power,' and as soon as the kundalini streams within you, your chakras begin opening up in succession.

Mastering Meditation

You can stop working at meditation if you approach the art with the wrong technique, and even by merely contacting the art without any strategy at all.

The direction you focus on also plays an essential role in the strategy of the Third Eye meditation method. Targeting your eyes straight outwards has to do with your conscious mind, while focusing downward relates to the subconscious mind.

When carrying out meditation, it is best to pick a position of your choice to meditate in. Traditionally, meditation is understood to be carried out in the lotus position. However, this position is not always a comfortable one, and so it is much better to be comfortable in another area of your own choice.

When you are choosing an area in which to perform your meditation, it is imperative that the excellent location is peaceful, and the very best option will, of course, be your cleaned and censed circle. If you select another area for whatever reason, it is best if you cleaned the city and get it censed as you did with your Circle. While it is not necessarily essential to face particular instructions in meditation, it is sometimes recommended to deal with the east. What is of many top priority is your comfort, and so if you have a much better view in other instructions, feel free to deal with that way rather!

With regards to the position you choose and the instructions you deal with as well as the area you select, you also are free to select the time of day you practice meditation. It is best to stick to that particular time of day every day to practice meditation so that your reflection is consistent. Thus, it is best to select the most convenient time, one that will be peaceful and peaceful; however, still achievable every day.

To remain active and succeed in meditation, it needs to be done consistently. Some suggest that meditation is performed between fifteen and twenty minutes a day, twice a day. At the bare minimum, you might

most likely manage with a single fifteen-minute session each day. Again, consistency is essential-- so it is essential to stay with the variety of courses and to the times also.

Performing Meditation

Step-By-Step Meditation Method

1. Position yourself well without bending your back.

2. Let your head roll forward onto your chest. Repeat three times.

3. Let your head roll backward. Take a deep breath in and out. Repeat three times. Go back to the initial standing position.

4. Let your head fall to the left as far as possible. Repeat three times.
5. Let your head fall to the right as far as possible. Take a deep breath in and out. Repeat three times. Return to the initial upright position.

6. Allow your head to fall forward again; today, move it counterclockwise in a circle. Repeat three times.

7. Let your head fall forward more, then move it clockwise in a circle. Repeat three times.

8. Breathe in some short intakes of breath, up until your lungs are filled, ensuring that you are breathing through your nose. Repeat three times.

9. Breathe wholly and slowly, in through the right nostril while holding the left closed. Enable your stomach to push out. Hold the breath briefly, and after that, exhale carefully and gradually from the mouth, flattening your stomach. This is a good exercise for removing stagnant air from the bottom of your lungs. Repeat three times.

10. Breathe slowly and totally, in through the left nostril while holding the left closed. Enable your stomach to balloon out. Hold the breath briefly, and then exhale carefully and gradually from the mouth, flattening your stomach. Repeat thrice.

Now that your body is well relaxed and you are breathing profoundly but usually focus the ideas in your mind and envision your whole body surrounded by a world of white light. Feel the energy in your entire body.

Now ensure you focus your attention on your toes. Relax them and feel the tension or the tiredness escape from them.

Relax your whole body entirely, focussing on releasing the tension from it a section at a time. Do not forget your eyes and even your scalp. The relaxation process is to end at your forehead.

Now, focus your energy on your 3rd eye. Permit your eyes to roll up if possible. Enable your energy to flow from inwards to outwards and to a higher power.

In the beginning, your conscious mind is unrestrained, and it may be difficult for you to quiet it, like a nagging child. However, with practice and consistency, you will ultimately begin to see outcomes in the form of a deepening in instinct, and this will be evidence of your Kundalini awakening.

It is not uncommon for novices to have trouble staying still in the beginning for more than a few minutes at any given time. It is usual for your mind to desire to roam and for you to feel like fidgeting. Very typical is the establishing of a massive itch that genuinely needs to be scratched! Overlook all these things as much as you can, and soon you will be in control of your mind and your body. It is a stringent process, but it is a transition from allowing your body and mind to rule over you, and now you attempt to rule over your body and mind.

Ending a Meditation Period

It is for the best interest of your physical well-being that you end each session of meditation by re-awakening your physical and conscious self. This is just done by carrying out the relaxation technique in reverse, which indicates pulling away from the pineal eye and continuing down the length of the body, section by section, making them each vibrant and awakened.

You may be amazed by how pleasant you will feel after you perform meditation using the proper strategy. Therefore there are not only spiritual benefits but physical also.

CHAPTER FIVE

Covens and Rituals

The Coven

There are mostly individual witches, and some witches choose to work in groups, which are designated as 'covens.' A coven is typically no more than thirteen, which is the conventional size of a coven, but it may be much smaller or larger than this.

Forming a Coven

The leaders of a coven are regarded as the priests of the coven. Such leaders have no more power than the others in the coven, but merely are leaders as all members of the coven get involved. According to your choice, those in your coven may be called their Witch name and 'Lad' or 'Lord' or only by their Witch name alone. Once again, it is a matter of choice.

There used to be one book per coven, but today it is not unusual for each Witch to own a personal Book of Shadows. Make one book for yourself from binding in any color of your choice and add pages of any style you choose, even crafting your paper from scratch if you would like. Fill the book with routines you want to carry out in your Circle and guarantee that it is written so plainly that you can read it in the candle.

The Initial Purification Ritual

This is to be carried out on the night of the New Moon.

1. Fill a flat bowl with water.

2. Kneel down and then place the water in front of you.

3. Place the forefinger of your right hand or left hand, if you happen to be left-handed into the water.

4. Visualize a brilliant beam of light streaming from the top and into the crown of your head. Imagine the shaft surging through your whole body and direct it through the arm you are using to reach the water. Picture the light spilling into the water through your finger.

5. Channel all the power you can into the water, with your eyes closed if it helps to focus.

Now shout out the following lines:

"Here do I purposefully direct my power, through the representatives of the God and the Goddess, into this water, that it might be clean and pure, as is my love for the Lord and Lady."

6. Take a teaspoon of sea salt; put it into the water and stir clockwise nine times with your finger. Chant the following three times:

"Salt is Life. Here is Life. Sacred and new; without strife."

7. Now put your fingers into the water and spray every corner of the temple room with the purified water. If there are cabinets or alcoves, sprinkle water in each of those corners, and chants the following mantras.

"Ever as I go through the ways, Do I feel the presence of the Gods. I understand that in aught, I do. They are with me

They abide in me.

And I in them, Forever

No evil shall be amused

For pureness is the resident

Within me and about me.

For great do I make every effort

And for great do I live—love unto all things.

Be it, Forever."

8. Next, it's time to light some incense. Take time to swing the burner in every corner, as was done with the sprinkling of the water. Repeat the following mantra three times:

"Salt is Life. Here is Life. Sacred and new; without strife."

The Sacred Circle.

Circles have been used in several religions and cultures faiths as a limit marking of sacred space, or as a classification of area for rites; rings keep the unwanted out and hold the wanted in the Circle. In Witchcraft, the Circle is a spiritual space within which the magickal power and energy are retained and concentrated.

There are instances in witchcraft when an exact Circle is required; however, that is just during Ceremonial Magick. Usually, accuracy is not required, but it is continuously good practice to show care abundantly and to do our best in making it as precise as possible. The measurements of the Circle being drawn depend on how many coven members will be within the circle and, likewise, the function of the ring. When magick is to be carried out within the circle, the sword needs to follow correctly on the right marking of the circle, and the enhancing of the energy in the Circle may even be carried out twice (but censing and spraying for the 2nd reinforcement is not needed).

The Circle Size.

What is most crucial when considering the actual size of the circle has to do with whether the ring comfortably fits the number of members that will be within it. Members ought to outstretch and move outwards up until their arms are extended to the optimum, and this has to be the ideal size of the Circle to be marked.

Drawing the Circle.

The illustration of the Circle must start at the east each time, and of course, end in the east. Outdoors; the circle can be marked with the point of a sword straight on the ground; While, when indoors, first mark the ring either with a cord, chalk, or even have a long-term marked circle on the ground if it is an irreversible temple ground. The marked circle is then charged with magickal energy or power by the Priest or Priestess walking the marking, directing his/her energy into the ring, using the sword's point.

On the Circle marking itself, erect four candles. The candles are explicitly positioned in the north, east, south, and west. For extra illumination or a preferred environment, other candles may be lit and placed in between these points, beyond the Circle.

Entry & Re-Entry of the circle during the working of Magick, it is vital that the Circle is not broken. In other instances, it is not chosen that any member leaves the Circle, but if it needs to be done, it is possible. There is a specific way by which the Circle is entered and left.

Leaving the Circle.

Position yourself in the East, with the athame held in hand. Make a move with the athame as though you plan to cut across the lines of the circle, starting on your right and then going to yours. You now might leave the Circle in between those lines. If preferred, you might picture a gateway that you have developed, in the east, through which you pass.

Re-entry of the Circle.

Need to you wish to return to the Circle, you go into through the very same gateway or doorway you think of that you have cut in the eastern side of the Circle. It is required to 'close' the opening behind you-- this is done by reconnecting the' cut' lines. When trying to reconnect the edges of the Circle, it is imperative to take note that three lines were in truth cut-- one that is made with the point of the sword, another made with the salted water and another made with the censing. Proceed to reconnect the lines by moving the athame blade across the borders up and down.

Kiss the tip of your athame and go back to your initial position in the Circle.

Clearing/ Setting up the Temple

This has to do with the opening and closing of the Circle, but can be referred to as the clearing and setting up of the Temple.

Erecting the Temple or Opening the Circle: This ritual is carried out at the beginning of every conference. Before building the temple, you will have your circle marked on the ground with candles at each quarter.

Step One: If your temple is not a permanent one, place a couple of altar candles, as per your choice, the incense burner, salt and water dishes, representations of the divine beings, anointing oil, goblets of white wine or juice, your tools, and the libation dish.

Step Two: In addition to the altar candles, the center lights the incense in the burner or thurible. At this moment, the four candles on the Circle are not yet lit. He then leaves the area to join the rest at the coven in north-eastern of the Circle.

Step Three: The designated priest and priestess go into the circle firstly and stand right before the altar. The priest then rings a bell, giving it three rings. The priest or priestess states the following:

"Be it understood that the Temple would be erected; the Circle is about to be cast. Let those who want attendance collect in the east and wait for the summons. Let no one be present here but of their own free choice."

Step Four: The priestess and the priest take the candle each, and they walk around the altar. Moving to the east. The priestess then lights the East candle on the circle from the lit altar candle she carries with her. As she lights the candle she states;

"Here, I bring air and light in at the east, to illuminate our temple and bring a breath of life."

Step Five: The priestess and priest light the south candle of the Circle, saying:

"Here, I bring fire and light in at the south, to illuminate our temple and make warmth available to it."

Step Six: The priestess and priest move west, where the priestess now lights the west candle, saying:

"Here, I bring water and light in at the west, to illuminate our temple and wash it."

Step Seven: The clergyman and priestess move north, where the north candle is lit by the priest, who states: "***Right here do I bring light and earth is at the north, to brighten our temple as well as to develop it in strength.***"

Step Eight: The priest and priestess moves to the east and back to the altar, finishing the Circle, and also changing the altar candles.

Step Nine: Either the priest or priestess lift the athame or sword and go back to the east. With the sword point on the eastern of the Circle, the priest or priestess progressively walks the solid line, focusing power and also power through his/her sword point into the Circle line.

Step Ten: Once done, he or she returns to the church. She or he ring the bell three times.

Step Eleven: The priest places the tip of his athame right into the salt and states: As salt is life, let it detoxify us in all ways we may use it. Allow it to clean our bodies and also spirits as we commit ourselves in these rites, to the splendor of the Goddess and the God.

Step Twelve: The priestess takes out the salt dish and also uses the tip of her athame to go down three stacks of salt right into the water. The priestess mixes the salted water with the same athame and also states*:*

Let the Sacred Salt drive out any type of contaminations in this water, that we may use it throughout these ceremonies.

Step Thirteen: The priest takes the scent heater while the priestess gets hold of the salted water. Each walk around the altar starting at the east, slowly strolling clockwise around the circle, with the Priest passing the incense along the significant ring, as well as the priestess scattering saltwater along the line. When they return to their beginning point at the east, they return to the altar and change the tools.

Step Fourteen: The priest and a pinch of the salt into the anointing oil, stirring it in with his finger. The priest blesses the priestess with the Keltic Cross in Circle if she is robed, or the Pentagram and Inverted Triangle if skyclad. He states*:*

In the name God and also the Goddess, I consecrate thee, bidding you welcome to this their Temple. They admire.

Step Fifteen: The priestess goes ahead to anoint the Priest with the oil and pronounces the very same words, adhered to by a salute. The priest and the priestess then move with each other to the eastern, with the priestess lugging the oil and the priest bringing his athame.

Step Sixteen: The priest makes two cuts throughout the line of the Circle with his athame, signifying the 'opening' of the Circle. The priestess anoints males, and the clergyman blesses women.

Be consecrated in the names of God and also the Goddess, bidding you welcome to this their Temple. Merry meet.

Step Seventeen: After the last participant goes enters, the priest shuts the Circle using his athame to cross throughout the line, connecting the 'damaged ends' of the Circle. The priest increases his athame and attracts a pentagram, sealing it. The priest and also priestess go back to the altar.

Step Eighteen: The priestess or priest states the following:

May you all be right here in tranquility as well as in love. We bid you welcome. Let now the Quarters be saluted and also the gods welcomed.

Step Nineteen: The member of the coven who is closest to the east turns outward faces the east candle of the Circle, elevating his/her athame. She or he draws an invoking pentagram, specifying:

All hail to the aspect of Air; Watchtower of the East. Might it stand in strength, ever before overseeing our Circle?

She or he kisses the blade of his/her athame and go back to the Circle.

Step Twenty: The participant of the coven closest to the south turns outside as well as bargains with the south candle of the Circle, elevating his/her athame. She or he draws a conjuring up pentagram, specifying:

All hail to the facet of Fire; Watchtower of the South. May it stand in stamina, ever seeing over our Circle.

She or he kisses the blade of his/her athame and also moves back to the Circle.

Step Twenty One: A member of the coven who is closest to the west turns outside and faces the Circle's west candle raising his/her athame. She or he attracts a conjuring up pentagram, stating:

All hailstorm to the element of Water; Watchtower of the West. May it stand in toughness, ever before managing the Circle.

He or she goes ahead to kiss the blade of his or her athame and goes back to the Circle in readiness for the next step.

Step Twenty-Two: A member of the coven closest to the north turns outside and also encounters the Circle's north candle, raising his/her athame. She or he draws an invoking pentagram, saying:

All hail storm to the facet of Earth; Watchtower of the North. May it stand in strength, ever before monitoring our Circle.

She or he kisses the blade of his/her athame and go back to the Circle.

Step Twenty-Three: The priestess or The priest elevates his/her athame and attracts a pentagram, specifying the following:

All hail the four Quarters and also all hail the Gods!

All coven participants sign up by saying, "***All hailstorm!***"

Step Twenty-Four: The priest or priestess states:

Let us share the Cup of Friendship.

The priest takes the goblet of red wine or juice and places a little directly onto the ground or into the libation dish, in the name of the gods. He takes the first sip and passes it to the priestess. The priestess takes a sip and also gives the cup to the coven member on her left. Therefore it continues till it is gone back to the altar. Bear in mind that it is the initial person who puts the drink just. The bell seems three times.

Step Twenty-Five: The priestess states: Now we are all here and is the Temple established up. Allow none leave, however, with superb reason, till the Temple is cleared. Mote It Be.

All participants repeat, "So Mote It Be!"

Clearing of the Temple or Closing of the Circle or This is carried out at the end of every conference;

Step One: The priest or priestess states: We came together crazy as well as relationship; allow us part the very same technique. Allow us to spread the love we have understood this Circle exterior to all, sharing it with those we meet.

The priest or priestess after that increases his athame or sword in salute. All participants then raise their athames.

Step Two: The clergyman or priestess states: Lord and also Lady, our thanks to you for sharing this moment. Our thanks for monitoring us, safeguarding, and

helping us in all points. Love is the Law, as well as Love, is the Bond. Merry did we meet; merry do we component; merry might we rejoin.

All members state: "Merry meet; jolly part; jolly reunite."

Step Three: The clergyman or priestess state: The Temple is currently gotten rid of.

Mote it be.

All members state: "So Mote It Be!"

Step Four: All members of the coven kiss their athame blades—participants after that walk the Temple to kiss each other farewell.

The Consecration Ritual

Your tools, as well as your priceless fashion jewelry, bring various vibrations in them, therefore prior to they can be used, it is needed that you execute an anointing ritual to commit them to your function of Witchcraft and also Magick and to clean them. The treatment is to spray and also to cense the items. Sea salt is initially charged with power and then blended with water to make what we can call 'Holy Water' for lack of a far better term. This water incorporated with the scent smoke act as spiritual, cleansing reps.

As soon as, Consecration of a product is done simply. The first action is to cast a Circle. Adhere to the routine and also presume as the action where you state: "Now is the holy place set up. I will certainly not leave it, however, with great factor. Be it."

Let's start from here, you proceed with the anointing routine as complies with: The

Consecration Ritual Step-by-Step

Hold the product you are consecrating up high in salute and also state: God and also

Goddess;

Lord as well as Lady;

Papa and Mother of All Life.

Below do I supply my device for your authorization.

From the materials of nature, it has been made; Wrought right into the kind you see now.

Place the product on your altar and kneel or mean a long time with your head bowed in respect as well as consideration over the building and construction of the product and also reviewing the little points you did to personalize the product.

Dip your fingers in the salty water and spray the product. Turn it over and also repeat

Get the item and also hold it in the scented smoke, engulfing it. State the following:

May the Sacred Water and also the smoke of the Holy Incense remove any kind of contaminants in this blade That it be cleansed and pure,

Prepared to offer me as well as my gods in any technique I choose. So mote it be.

Holding the item in your hands direct all the energy you can muster towards the product.

With the knowledge as well as might of the God and also Goddess.

Might it serve us well, maintaining me from injury, as well as acting in their solution, in all things?

Mote it be.

Shut the Circle by elevating the now consecrated thing in your right-hand man, as well as state the following: My thanks to the gods for their involvement.

May they ever before monitor me, safeguarding and also assisting me in all that I do Love is the Law, as well as Love, is the Bond.

Be It.

The routine is now total. You require to keep the product on your individual for twenty-four hours after the method and also copulate the item underneath your cushion for three nights straight. Nobody is to obtain your product for usage, whether within or out of the Circle, though it could be held, touched as well as looked at by them.

CHAPTER SIX

The Principles Of The Craft As It Relates To Birth, Death & Marriage

Marriage in Wicca

In Wiccan belief, instead of a marital relationship like that of Christendom, where a couple is bound for the period of their lives up until "death do us part," the Wiccan wedding is one that dedicates a man and woman to each other only for as long as they like each other. If it occurs that they, later on, find they have fallen out of love with each other, the man and woman easily separate without any threat of 'sin' or the like. This is a convenient arrangement as relationships often progress, and nobody desires to be forced into remaining with a partner they no longer want to be with.

The Wiccan marriage ceremony is called the Handfasting Ceremony.

In modern times, the majority of individuals prefer to draw up their own Handfasting rites.

Here we will supply the Seax-WiccaHandfasting rite as a standard-- feel free to either follow the rituals as they are or to use them as a standard for developing your own Handfasting rite.

Seax-WiccaHandfasting Rite

The ideal time for performing the Wiccan marriage ceremony is actually during the waxing of the Moon. It is good to have flowers decorating the Altar and the inside of the Circle, if possible. It is likewise more suitable for all coven members to be skyclad for the Handfasting rite.

If the particular coven is usually robed and does not wish to be skyclad, it is recommended that at least the Bride and the Groom be skyclad throughout the rite.

Much like the 'conventional' marriage being held in modern times, so too are rings exchanged in the Seax-Wiccan standard wedding. The rings are typically bands crafted from gold or silver and inscribed with the Bride and Groom's witch names on the rings in runes. At the start of the rite, these rings are to rest at the Altar, with The Priapic Wand.

The Handfasting Rite Step-By-Step-Perform the Opening of the Circle orSetting up of the Temple.

The priest and priestess kiss; A coven member then says: There are those in our midst who seek the bond of Handfasting.

The Priestess then says, "Let them be named and brought forward."

The coven member responds with," [Groom's witch name] is the Man and[Bridetobe's witch name] is the Woman."

The woman and man in question move across the Altarto stand to face the priest and priestess, with the Groom opposite the priestess and the Bride opposite the priest

The Priestess asks the Groom, "Why are you here?"

The groom responds., "IwishaHandpartingfrom[Wife's name]"

The Priestess asks, "What is your desire?".

The groom shares, "To be made one with [Bride-to-be's name], in the eyes of the Gods and the Wicca."

Now the Priest relies on the Bride. He asks, "Are you [name]."

The Bride reacts, "I am.".

The Priest asks, "What is your desire?".

The Bride answers, "To be made one with [Groom's name], in the eyes of the gods and the Wicca.".

The Priestess grabs the sword and raises it high. The Priest hands over the Priapic Wand to the Bride and Groom, who hold it with both sides between them.

The Priestess states, "Lord and Lady, here before you stand two of your folk. See, now, that which they have to declare."

The Priestess places the sword back onto the Altar, takes her athame, and then holds the tip of it to the chest of the Groom.

She says to the Groom: "Repeat after me:

'I [Groom's name], do come here of my own free choice, to look for the partnership of [Bride's name] I add all love, honor, genuineness, wanting just to turn into one with her whom I like. Continually will I strive for [Bride-to-be's name]'s joy and well-being. I will defend her life before mine. May the athame be plunged into my heart if I am not sincere in all.

I swear this all in the names of the gods. May they offer me the strength to keep my oath.

The Priest lowers his athame, and the Priestess takes the rings from the Altar and sprays them both with salted water and census them with the thurible. She then passes the Bride's ring to the Groom and the Groom's ring to the Bride. The man and woman take them in their right-hand, holding the Priapic Wand with their left.

The Priest states: As the grass of the fields and the trees of the woods flex together under the pressures of the storm, so too must you both bend when the wind blows strong. As you provide love, so will you get strength.

The Priestess then says: Know you that no two people can be exactly alike. There will be some periods when it will seem harsh to give and to love diligently. See then your reflection as in a forest pool: when the image you see looks irate and unfortunate, then is the time for you to smile and to love (for it is not fire that puts out the light).

The Priest then states: Ever love, help and respect each other, And then know sincerely that you are one in the eyes of the gods and of the Wicca.

All coven members state, "So Mote It Be!".

The Priest then takes the Priapic Wand from the Bride and Groom and returns it to the Altar. The Groom and Bride then kiss the Priest and the Priestess across the Altar and move around the Circle to accept congratulations from the coven members.

Handparting Rite

Many faiths see marriage as a one-time lifetime commitment, indicating the couple are to stay together no matter the conditions or circumstances and even if they don't love each o the many more.

In the Wiccan belief, casual partnerships are not encouraged, but it is accepted that with time, relationships change, and husband and wife may no longer be happy being together later. After all attempts at salvaging the relationship are first made, then the last hope is a Handparting event, which can be likened to a divorce.

Before carrying out the rite, the partner and wife sit with the Priest and Priestess to come up with reasonable departments of their possessions and to organize assistance for kids if there are any. Ascribe is available to record everything. If either of the lovers can not be available for whatever reason, their position might be represented by another Witch of the same sex if there is a signed agreement from the missing party, and the wedding event ring.

The Handparting Rite Ste-By-Step

- The Opening of the Circle or Erecting of the Temple is performed.
- The Priestess and Priest Kiss.
- A coven member then says, " [Other half's name] and [Spouse's name], stand forth.".

- The spouses move forward to stand before the Altar, with the Husband in front of Priestess, and the Wife in front of Priest.

- Priestess asks the Husband, "Why are you here?".

  The Husband answers, "I want a Handparting from [Partner's name] The Priest now asks the Wife, "Why are you here?".

  The Wife responds with, "I wish a Handparting from [Other half's name].

- The Priestess asks them both, "Do you both desire this of your own free choice?".

The couple responds with, "We do.".

- The Priest asks, "Has a settlement been reached between you relating to the sharing of property and care of the children?".

The Husband and Wife react, saying, "It has.".

- The Priest asks, "Has this been appropriately recorded, signed, and also witnessed?".

  Now the covener Scribe verifies, saying, "It has.".

- The Priest then says, "Then let us proceed, keeping in mind that we stand ever before the gods.".

- The Husband and the Wife join hands and then repeat the following together, line by line, after the Priestess:

  "I, [Name], do at this moment most freely dissolve my union with [Spouse's name], and I do so in all honesty and genuineness, before the gods, with my brothers and sisters of the Craft as witnesses. To one another, let all ties be loose, but ever will we maintain respect for one another, as we have love and regard for our fellow Wiccans.

- The Priest then makes the announcement, "Hand part!".

- The couple releases their hands earlier joined together, remove their rings, and give to the Priestess. The Priestess sprays the rings and census them. The Priestess then specifies, "In the names of the Gods do I clean these rings.".

- The priestess then returns the cleansed rings to the man and lady to do with them as they please.

- The Priestess states, "Now are you handpainted. Let all understand you as such. Split in your diverse ways in Peace and Love-- never in bitterness-- and in the ways of the Craft. Mote, it be."

All coven members repeat, "So mote it be.".

- After the routine, follows Ale ritual and Cakes, then cleaning of the Temple or closing of the Circle.

Birth Rite-- Wicanning.

Witches don't believe in coercing or forcing the Craft on anybody, not even their children. Children are taught the methods of the Craft and may also be initiated when they are old enough to make their choice, and they might then either continue practicing the Craft or give it up. No second initiation is required if they resume the Craft later.

A ritual is generally carried out for a kid for the parents to ask the gods to monitor them, protect them, and assist them. The routine may be performed at any time, at any other ritual, and even on its own. Similar to any ritual, first is the erecting of the Temple, then the routine, then the Cakes and Ale and the Clearing of the Temple.

The Birth Rite Step by Step

- The Priestess and Priest kiss.
- A coven member states: "There is an addition to our number. Let us give her/him due welcome.".
- The parents of the beginner position themselves across the Priest and Priestess, on the other side of the Altar, holding the child to be started.
- The Priest asks, "What is the name of the child?".
- The mother and father of the child then supply a name by which the child shall be known within the Circle till that time, the child might choose to adopt a new name when older.
- The Priest then says, "We welcome you [Name]."
- The Priestess states, "Welcome, and much love to you.".

- The Priest and the Priestess then proceed to lead the kid's parents clockwise around the circle three times. The Parents then hold the kid above the Altar, as though 'using' the child.

- The parents then state, "We here offer the fruit of our love to the gods. May they guide her/him as s/he grows.".

- The Priestess then dips the tips of her fingers in the salted water, then wipes them carefully across the kid's face. The mother then passes the baby through the incense smoke to cense the baby.

- The Priestess then mentions, "May the Lord and the Lady ever smile upon you.".

- The Priest states, "May they protect you and assist you through this life.".

- The Priestess states, "May they help you select that which is ideal and shun that which is wrong.".

- The Priest states, "May they see that no damage befalls you, or others through you.".

- The Priestess then states to the parents of the child, "We charge you both, in the names of the God and of the Goddess, to lead this kid, by teaching the way of crafting with love and how to honor them by harming none..".

- The Priest then specifies: "Teach him/her of the Lord and the Lady; of this life, of all that preceded and what might follow after. Tell the stories of the gods and teach the history of our Craft. Teach her/him to aim for that perfection which all desire and, when the time is right, hope-- but do not press-- that s/he accompanies us and becomes genuinely among our precious household."

- The mother and father then specify, "All this we will do. So do we pledge.".

- The Priest and Priestess then state together: "We bid welcome to [Name]."

- All coven members then mention, "Welcome!".

* Now follows the path of Cakes and Ale ceremony.

Death Rite-- Crossing the Bridge.

This might be done as a rite in and of itself, in which case it is preceded by the Erecting of the Temple and followed by Cakes and Ale then Clearing of the Temple. If carried out during other routines, it needs to be carried out before Cakes and Ale rite.

- The Priestess and Priest kiss

- Using the horn, a long note is sounded when, by a coven member.

- A coven member states, "The horn is sounded for [Name of departed Witch].

All coven members respond with, "So be it.".

- The priestess then states, "That today [Name] is not with us, here in the Circle, saddens us all. Let us try not too heartbroken. For is this not to show that s/he has fulfilled this life's work? Now is s/he free to move on. We will reunite, never to be afraid. And that will be a time for another event.".

- The Priest then includes, "Let us send out forth our good dreams to bear him/her across the Bridge. May s/he return any moment s/he may want, to be with us here.".

- All members of the coven grab their athames, pointing them at a position behind the Altar, while facing the Priest and the Priestess.

- All members imagine, in their mind's eye, the image of the deceased Witch, as though she is basing on the spot. The members concentrate on carrying pleasure, joy, and love from their innermost being, through the line of their athame and out of the point into the envisioned body.

- This continues for a couple of moments. Completion is indicated by the Priestess when she changes her athame and states: "We sincerely wish you all the Love and Happiness. We will never forget you. Do not forget us. Whenever we meet here, your presence is always welcome.".

- All coven members then finish by saying, "So mote it be.".

- Now all coven members sit. If there be any member who desires to say a couple of words concerning the departed, they might do so. If there is nobody happy to do so, the

Priest or Priestess must speak kind reminiscent words of the departed Witch, explicitly focusing on happy moments.

- Cakes and Ale event follow the rite.
-
-

CHAPTER SEVEN

Love and Sex Magick

Concepts of magick involve timing and feeling.

Timing &Magick: As you may not currently understand, the phase of the Moon is essential in working magic properly. The two main aspects of the moon are the "Waxing Moon and the Waning Moon."

Feeling &Magick: As was pointed out in the intro to spells and charm, a deep-set psychological desire for something to happen is essential for magick to be efficient. Putting every minute of your presence into wanting the magick to work is the fuel that drives your magick. Rhyme and chant are tools for magnifying the power of your desire. The balanced chanting serves to increase your sensations and assists you focus on your appetite better. Dance is another amplifier, which can help raise the power behind your magick. Sex is long considered a natural powerhouse for magick, and more will be discussed on sex magick later in this chapter.

Preparing Your Body for Magick

Having a clean body is very crucial before working magick. A tidy collection is accomplished through both external and internal cleaning. Bathing the body is, of course, the initial step, and it is suggested to include a teaspoon of sea salt to the bathing water for cleansing possessions. The inner body is prepared by abstaining from alcohol, sex, and nicotine. This is to be done as a twenty-four-hour quick before you mean to work magick.

The Moon &Magick

Constructive and Destructive Magick

The two words of the moon identify what kind of magick is to be appropriately carried out. Throughout the waxing moon, constructive magick is carried out. Constructive magick includes rituals and spells based on love, security, health, fertility, and success. Naturally, then, during the waning moon, harmful magick is performed, like magick based upon elimination, separation, and extermination, or the casting of binding spells.

Love Magick

This magick is intended for long-term soul mate looking for future partners and is not intended for finding somebody to have a casual affair with. Possibly one of the categories of magick that produces the most interest is love magic when it comes to magick. There is much interest in love potions and love philters, though most of the attention is rooted in fiction. Some love magick spells do work, like the magick, including'poppets.' Poppets are used to represent the enthusiasts that are in concern, and the idea is that whatever is done to the poppets is done unto the enthusiasts.

The poppet is a specially ready doll made from cloth, even if it is a rough cut figure. While eliminating the fabric and preparing the poppet, it is crucial to be conscious of the individual the doll that is being developed is planned to represent. The baby might be made as elaborately as preferred, such as; embroidery, beadwork and facial functions, etc. are all acceptable. Make the poppet from two pieces of cloth and leave the leading open so it may be packed with herbs. The poppets are to be packed with vervain, verbena, feverfew, yarrow, Artemesia, valerian, rosebuds, motherwort, damiana, or elder, as they are all herbs governed by Venus. Once stuffed, the top may be stitched to seal.

Prepare two poppets in this manner, one male and one female. The preparation is all carried out within the spiritual Circe, and it may be carried out by a singular witch or all coven members.

Since it is an ideal mate that is being looked for, the second figure is to be made with all the qualities desired in them. The poppet is nameless; however, it can display all physical desires and attributes. Once prepared, the poppets lay on the altar, with one at the left-hand side of the sword and the other on the right-hand side. The poppets are to be placed in front of the sword. On the altar, there is to lay a red ribbon, 21 inches long. The petitioner then states,

"O magnificent God and Goddess, Hear now my plea to you.

My plea for real love for [name] and for his/her desire."

The Petitioner then gets the proper poppet and sprinkles the poppet with salted water and cleanses it thoroughly. While doing this, the petitioner states,

"I call this Poppet [petitioner's name] It is him/her in all ways. As she exits, so exists this poppet. Aught that I fix to it, I fix to her."

The petitioner then changes the poppet, to pick up the other one. Just like the previous, it is sprinkled and censed, and the petitioner states,

"This poppet is her preferred mate in every way. As he exits, so exists this poppet. Aught that I fix to it, I fix to him too.".

The petitioner changes the poppet and moves to kneel before the altar with one hand on each poppet. At the point that the poppets fulfill, the petitioner might open his/her eyes and, while holding the poppets deal with to face still, state:

"Thus may they be drawn.

One to the other, Strongly and genuinely.

To be together always.

As One.

No more will they be separated; No more alone, But ever quick together.

As One.".

The poppets need to be laid together on the altar, in the center, with the sword across them, on top of them. The petitioner or the whole coven might now dance around them and work magick for ten minutes, directing the energy of their tune and dance to bring the two represented individuals together. Alternatively, all may sit and meditate on the idea of the two represented coming together.

This routine is best performed on three consecutive Fridays throughout the waxing moon, or maybe even on a Friday, Wednesday then Friday. The complete ritual is meant to be played as almost to the Full Moon as is possible.

On the final Friday, the Petitioner says,

"Now might the Lord and the Lady bind these two together, as I do bind them here.".

The poppets are used up and bound with red ribbon many times around both the poppets, tying the ends together around them. The petitioner then states,

"Now are they forever one, even as the Gods themselves. May each become a part of the other that, separated, they would be incomplete. So Mote It Be!".

As soon as again positioned below the sword and left for some time while the petitioner carries out meditation, the bound poppets are. As soon as the ritual is finished, the poppets are to be covered in a clean white cloth and after that stored thoroughly, never to be unbound.

Sex Magick

Sex magick is an extremely potent form of magick as it is dealing with life forces. Sex magick is about using the power of the orgasm and using that and the entire sexual experience for magickal functions.

i. All aspects of extrasensory understanding to be increased in the course of sexual excitation.

ii. The mind is to be in a state of hypersensitivity before, throughout, and after the climax.

iii. The consistency of peak sexual sensations aids access to the world of the unconscious.

iv. During the height, an experience of timelessness or overall ego dissolution might be experienced, and feelings of being' soaked up' by the sexual partner.

The act of sexual relations is the most natural approach to generate the power required to perform practical magick. The entire process of copulation follows the procedure of beginning slowly and a progressive building up, increasing in rhythm until the final climactic explosion. This act may be carried out within the circle either by a couple or by the whole coven, or even by a solitary witch.

Start as usual, with a period of meditation to focus on what you prefer to accomplish. Take up positions in couples and kneel facing one another. The item is to attain sexual stimulation, and this might be carried out for as long as it is needed and not to be rushed through.

The focus is now to be concentrated on the object of the magick, the function for which it is being carried out. This shift in focus might also assist in delaying climax. This is the time in which both the male and lady fix in their minds an image of the desire and concentrate their energies on it. Feel the power construct.

When the male understands he can not resist the urge to orgasm, he can throw himself back to lie flat on the flooring and launch the power that constructed within him as he climaxes. He must see the power flashing as white light in a line. On climax, she too will fall forwards to lie over her sexual partner.

Obviously, for the singular witch, the act is performed through masturbation, and the longer the orgasm can be held off, the more power is created for completing the magick. For couples, mutual masturbation or foreplay are two alternatives, both producing intense energy.

CHAPTER EIGHT

Quartz Crystal

Crystal, quartz is the second most plentiful mineral in the world, and among the most common stones, you will find in magical supply stores.

Comprised of just two aspects-- silicon and oxygen, it runs in different colors from entirely "clear" to milky white. Clear quartz is discovered as a six-sided prism and is often used in schools to demonstrate the capability of a mineral to hold the whole spectrum of light, kept in the sunshine; the crystal will transfer rainbow patterns onto floors and walls.

The Aztecs, Egyptians, Romans, and lots of other ancient cultures used quartz in a multitude of ways that varied from meditations to funerary rituals, which may have simulated the moonlight shining down on the individuals.

Some understood it as "the Witch's mirror," quartz is connected with both the Moon and the Sun and the Elements of Water and Fire. This stone is a powerful tool for saving energy in the means of thoughts, emotions, and memories, and can be easily "programmed" to activate previously stored energy when hired. Quartz is often used to charge excellent tools and spell components, and can even be used to clean different stones and crystals energetically.

Quartz is also referred to as the "sage" of most minerals as it highly assists with the combining of the spiritual and physical worlds.

Quartz sends and absorbs energy from the Sun as well as from the vital force of plants, flowers, and trees, and like several other crystals, it can be used to rejuvenate struggling plants around the home. Quartz is a fantastic all-around rebalancing stone, changing unfavorable energies with positive ones and keeping harmonious vibrations going strong in any location where it lives.

In this chapter, you'll discover how to use quartz for storing and recovering memories, stimulating divination tools, improving your health, and increasing your energy towards attaining a particular objective.

Crystal Divination Recalibration

Quartz is often used to charge routine and beautiful tools. As a stone of spiritual interaction and psychic ability, it's ideal for improving your divination tools, such as Tarot cards, runes, a pendulum, etc., whenever you can notice their energy has ended up being "fuzzy" or imbalanced in some way. To keep the power-up, the Tarot specialists keep the quartz crystal and cards together. Technically, it is your choice to use any crystal size with any kind of foretelling tools, but it's finest to "match" the two as closely as possible. For instance, a small crystal point may work well when rebalancing a pendulum, but when it concerns a Tarot deck or bag of runes, a more sizable crystal is perfect. You will require:

- One medium to a big quartz crystal
- White candle
- Divination tool(s).

Guidelines:

- Light the candle and invest a couple of moments, silencing your mind.
- When you're ready, put the divination tool in your left hand and the quartz in your right hand.
- Gently bring them together up by colliding them.
- Hold both for at least 1 minute, picture the divination tool being cleared of any unwanted energy, and then renewed using pure quartz energy.
- When you notice the recalibration is done, give thanks to the quartz and place your prophecy tool on the altar.
- Repeat the treatment with any other prophecy tools you wish to rebalance. Gently snuff out the white candle when you have completed it.

Crystal Quartz Memento Charm.

As computer system researchers have been finding, quartz can save info, or "data," in the type of energy. However, it likewise stores emotional info that makes this crystal an exceptional touchstone for pleasant memories that you wish to keep. This spell is an excellent one to explore the energetic properties of quartz. Simply pick a pleasant memory, whether current or from the remote past, and charge the stone with the sensations it highlights in you.

Keep in mind: this works best with pure, clear quartz, so look for as clear stone as possible.

You will need:

- One clear quartz crystal.
- White, pink, or yellow candle.
- Journal or writing paper (optional).

Guidelines:

- Light the candle and invest a long time silencing your mind.
- Start to remember the memory in as much information. You may wish to spend 10 to 15 minutes thinking about it; if it is a memory of a past event, this is guaranteed to raise information you might not be able to gain access to otherwise.

- When you have an excellent grasp on the memory, take the quartz and hold it between your palms.
- With your eyes closed, picture every possible sensory detail about the memory, sights, sounds, tastes, noises, voices, your ideas and sensations at the time, and so on. Concentrate on the feelings that accompanied this memory and feel them again in the present moment.
- Continue to visualize until you feel the warm and positive energy. Then place the flint in front of the candle, leaving it for at least an hour.
- You can now hold the quartz when you want to come into contact with this memory and feel the positive feelings with which you have soaked the stone. You can put it on your altar or any other place where you see it often or carry it with you in your pocket or purse.

Crystal Elixir for Physical Health.

Crystal elixirs, the infusing of water with the vibrations of crystals and other mineral stones, have been used for healing purposes since 3000B.C.E. in numerous cultures. These essential, wonderful potions work through the body's direct absorption of the vibrations of the crystal, creating an alignment between your energy which of the stone picked for the specific purpose.

The quartz power of rebalancing can be used to produce physical regeneration and revitalization in the body by working at the subtle energy level. This elixir is excellent for those who have been feeling short on energy, are recuperating from a minor illness, or would merely like a well-rounded rebalancing "lift" of recovery energy.

Keep in mind: Some stones and crystals are highly hazardous, and need not to be used internally in any method. So if you desire to explore this particular magical method, even more, be sure to do extensive research on any stone you're considering for usage in an elixir!

You will need:

- One little piece of clear quartz.
- A cup of filtered water.

Directions:

- Put the quartz in a little glass of water and leave it in the sunshine for one day. The following day, carry out the ritual healing.
- Carefully remove the quartz from the water and place it on your altar or table.
- Keep the water in the middle of your altar or table.
- Relax and focus by taking three deeper breath

- Take a moment to practice meditation on your body. Let your mind explore your body from top to bottom. Report any place that may require attention.
- Go back to the top place you noticed an imbalance in your body. Concentrate on recovery that is happening and be sipping a glass of water.
- Picture the ancient wisdom and power of the quartz healing that point, releasing any stress, discomfort, or other unwanted feelings.
- Practice this method with any of the body part that needs healing. Permit yourself a minute to feel the vibration of the when you are ended quartz throughout your body, healing and restoring your being.
- You can duplicate this ritual whenever your body requires a boost of recovery energy.

EnergyAmplifierforReachingaGoal

Quartz serves as a power amplifier that aid in achieving a goal. When the heart is set on a specific objective, quartz is a useful magical ally to assist you in crystallizing your will and intent. Whether it's related to affection, career, health, or spiritual development, quartz can accelerate the fulfillment of your desires by enhancing the energy that is set into it.

As you perform this spell, it is necessary to not just think about the end outcome of your goal; however, to direct the energies of sensation pleased and successful with your sign into the stone. You will need:

- One pure, clear quartz crystal.
- Little slip of paper.
- Little drawstring bag.

Instructions:

- Invest some time silencing your mind.
- Concentrate on the goal you have produced yourself.
- Write your objective on the small slip of paper. Remember to be very particular about what you would like to obtain, as this will assist in concentrating the energy on the result you want.
- Use a slip of paper to wrap the quartz
- Ensure you are holding both the quartz and paper in your hand.

- Focus on your goal by envisioning it being completed. How will you feel? What effects or impacts will lead to your life?
- When you have fortified the most detailed and positive visualization possible, place the paper quartz in a sliding

bag and insert it saying the following words (or comparable):

"With the stone of earth and the power of fire. I express the desire of my heart. "

- Put the quartz where it can be close to you in your activities to reach the goal. It could be on your desk, in your purse, in your vehicle, on your computer system, or in a space in your home.
- Repeat this spell with new quartz and a new objective whenever you require it.

Rose Quartz.

Extensively love for its joyful yet relaxing pink shades, increased quartz gets its color from trace quantities of iron, manganese or titanium found within what would otherwise be clear or white quartz. This is another commonly abundant mineral that can be discovered in any magical supply shop, and is frequently made into pendants, rings, pendants, and other fashion jewelry.

Archeological records back to 800 BC reveal that increased quartz was used in jewelry and cosmetics by the Assyrians, Greeks, and Romans. The ancient Egyptians stated that the goddess Isis rubbed rose quartz on her cheeks and around her eyes to protect her appeal. This skin-care technique was a long-held custom in Egypt, and now that crystals have seen a renewal in interest over some years, it has just recently returned into style in the West!

The color pink is believed to be the best symbol for love and empathy, and it can be used for all magical operations associating with these qualities. Many call it the Love Stone, rose quartz opens the heart chakra to allow love to permeate our lives. It aids in healing psychological injury, animosities, regret, and anger.

There is a relationship between water, venus and earth element, as they increased quartz assists to raise self-esteem and self-regard by reminding us to treat ourselves with gentle forgiveness and compassion, and is a very efficient crystal to use during meditation. Increased quartz improves one's inner awareness, teaching us that unconditional love is ever-present, and we just need to be open to receiving the healing energies of the Universe.

Home Energy Transformation Spell

All homes need fairly routine energetic upkeep for the atmosphere to stay perfect. Rose quartz is uniquely fit for this work, as it can replace unfavorable energy with positive energy. This spell will assist you to clean out and repair any pockets of harmful or otherwise undesirable energy in your house. You will be replacing these unfavorable energies with the warm, earthy glow of peace, well-being, and groundedness.

Keep in mind: This spell is powerful on its own, however for even higher effect, attempt sweeping and smearing your house with sage before you start.

You will need:

- One medium to big increased quartz crystal per space or location.
- White candle (optional).

Directions:

- Put the candle at the center of your house and light it if using. Spend a few minutes silencing your mind.
- find a room that is very comfortable fo you
- Place the rose in your hand, focusing on the cold, positive sensation it discharges.
- Now put it on the floor in front of you and visualize pink light radiating outward from the crystal, spreading throughout the space.
- Feel any negative energy being changed by a soothing, caring vibration from the rose quartz.
- When you feel the energy is sufficiently changed, state these words:

" light and lover are constantly present in this area. All is well.".

- Now pick the quartz up and put it in a safe area room for a continuation of the energy balance.
- Do the ritual again in any room that has unwanted vibrations.

Spell to Release Pain and Unexpressed Emotions.

Often we are not able to express emotions in particular situations or don't have the words to reveal our feelings. Stifling our souls in this method can be an excellent short-term defense reaction, but ultimately it will become a source and fester of unattended negativeness.

Releasing these unpleasant feelings will enable you to process grief or trauma, heal from emotional injuries, and clear your heart space so that you are open to receive love and compassion from deep space and others in your life. This routine can be used for healing from specific past emotional wounds, or for merely clearing more basic psychological clutter from your energy field.

You will need:

- One rose quartz crystal.
- Pink spell candle.
- Lavender necessary oil (optional).

Directions:

- Light the candle and shut your mind in a few minutes
- Use the left hand to hold the quartz. (The left hand enables energy to flow straight to your heart center.) To increase the strength of the spell, you can keep the rose quartz over your heart.
- For 3 minutes, allow your ideas to stream naturally, requesting for anything that needs to be launched to come into your awareness.
- Do not hold on to any specific thought, instead, feel it, accept it, and let it move through you. Offer the crystal your approval to recover and relieve you by radiating love and understanding throughout your body.

- As you breathe, breathe in the soothing essence of the rose quartz, and exhale to allow any stuck energy from past discomfort and trauma to be free.
- Use a lavender oil to anoint the quartz rose by applying one to two drops
- Then bury it in the Earth to clean it from the energies of the old feelings. Leave it there for one whole night.
- You can recycle the stone as frequently as required.

Shining Light Self-Love and Self-confidence Spell

In a society intense on materialism and surface area appearances, the concepts of "self-love" and "self-esteem" can be complicated. Often people want their skills and achievements for sources of self-acceptance, but this technique is missing out on the point entirely.

Real self-love comes from within, when we acknowledge that we are divine beings of light no matter how we appear or what we do (or don't do) in the outside world. Anyone battling with insecurities or self-acceptance needs this spell. Is your choice to practice this spell with a rose quartz or bracelet for an easily-wearable appeal.

You will require:

- One rose quartz crystal (or increased quartz locket/ bracelet).
- One pink candle.
- One orange candle.

Guidelines:.

- Put the rose quartz between the two candles.
- Take a minute to quiet your mind, and after that light, the pink candle, proclaiming these words:

" the light is staring at shines as the love I have for myself shine."

- Now turn on the orange candle, saying the following words:

" This light shines as my self-expression shines.".

- Choose rose quartz and hold it between your palms.
- For a moment, focus on the light shining on the candles and feel the love that comes from the stone in your hands.
- Take a deep breath, close your eyes, and repeat the following words seven times:

" I accept myself. I trust myself. I love myself. From within, I shine for all the".

- Gently snuff out the candles world to see.
- Wear or go around with the rose quartz every day till you feel more rooted in your confident sense of self.
- If you feel the need, you can duplicate the spell occasionally to charge the stone.

Spell To Attract Positive Relationships.

"like attracts like," this is what we learn from the law of attraction and that what we think of identifies what we bring into our experience. This holds in all areas of life but is often most clearly seen when it concerns relationships. Do you feel you are dating the wrong individuals, or discover yourself surrounded by bonds that aren't satisfying, you require to move your energetic vibration to turn this pattern around.

This is much easier said than done; however, if you do not have a great deal of experience with positive, healthy relationships. Whether you're seeking a new buddy or a romantic partner, or both, this spell helps you open yourself as much as assistance from deep space.

You will require:

- Two little increased quartz crystals.
- One pink or white candle.

- Two pieces of writing paper.
- Fire-resistant meal.

Instructions:

- Light the candle and put one increased quartz on either side of it. Take a few minutes to silent the mind.
- On the very first paper, make a note of the qualities of relationships and romantic relationships that have been unhealthy for you in your life. Do not use names or focus on specific people, but rather strive to articulate the actions that have injured you and the resulting feelings from these encounters.
- Do not stay too much on any single incident or individual, and don't enter into more detail than necessary, the point is not to reinforce the unfavorable experiences, but just to recognize and acknowledge what it is that you want to be devoid of in your life.
- When you're through, tear the paper up into a few pieces, and spark them one at a time on the candle flame, taking care not to burn your fingers.
- Drop them into the fire-resistant meal and let them stress out.
- Pick the second paper to compose about what you want to manifest in your future relationship(s). Let the Universe

know what you require in terms of aid in moving these patterns in your life.

- Fold the paper four times and position it in front of the candle when you're finished.
- Place a paper and put the crystals on it and state the following words:

"As I value myself, I bring in others who do the very same.

Let it be.".

- Leave the candle to stretch itself.
- Bury the ashes of burnt paper or scatter them on Earth.
- Keep a folded paper in your magazine, Book of Shadows, or elsewhere, you might call a "list" for the next few weeks and months as new people come into your life.
- If you like, take the crystals with you in your purse or pocket when you go out.

Amethyst.

Another variation of quartz, this magnificent crystal is available in different shades of purple, from pale lavender to lilac and purple. The color is triggered by manganese and iron present in the clear quartz. Many geodesspherical rocks with crystal-lined hollow cavities, add amethyst and clear quartz points clustered together. Amethyst is also sometimes discovered with citrine in the very same crystal. This mix is called ametrine. Amethyst is a relatively abundant mineral. However, the most significant deposits are found in Mexico, Brazil, Uruguay, Russia, France, and parts of Northern and Southern Africa.

In the ancient world, amethyst was mostly understood as a stone that could prevent drunkenness, which we can see in the Greek origins of the name, which equates to "not intoxicate." While it's uncertain precisely why the ancients associated this power to amethyst, they should have sensed its high vibrational frequency, as even today, this crystal is used in alternative recovery to assist with healing from dependency.

Associated with the world Jupiter and the Element of Air, amethyst has a history of helping bring calm and balance to the emotional, physical, and spiritual worlds. It has been known to assist individuals carefully resolve their grief, tame their emotions, and move the previous suffering. It can also push back emotional outbursts and eliminate antagonistic and confrontational attitudes, making it useful in wonderful workings connected to solving disputes of all kinds, even in legal matters. This crystal truly radiates relaxing energy, as anybody who uses amethyst or keeps it around the house can confirm!

The spells listed below make use of the energies of amethyst to assist you in conquering addiction, cultivate persistence and flexibility, smooth over legal trouble, and secure yourself from theft while traveling.

Ritual to Break Free of Addiction.

Amethyst's tranquil, yet highly powerful energies are extensively used in spells, routines, and alternative recovery modalities to treat dependencies of all kinds. This routine concentrates the residential or commercial properties of amethyst into a helpful and protective talisman for you to keep with you as needed to help you stay out of old, unwanted habits.

The "amulet" stated can be a locket, bracelet, ring or anklet with a minimum of one amethyst stone in it, but you can also create your own by wrapping an amethyst securely with yarn, precious jewelry, or twine wire and affixing it to a chain or cord. Many crystal stores also sell pendants with small wire "baskets" into which any stone can be placed.

Remember: if you are not having a good time with a dependency on drugs, alcohol, or disordered consuming habits that presents a risk to your health, please do not count on this spell alone to solve the issue. Instead, believe it as a compelling action along the course to your recovery.

You will need:.

- One amethyst amulet.
- Black or violet candle.
- Two papers.
- Fireproof dish.

Guidelines:

- Light the candle and spend some time silencing your mind. When you feel centered, compose a list of the unfavorable impacts of your routine or dependency on the first paper.
- Hold the stone of the amulet in between your palms, close your eyes, and take three deep breaths, visualizing yourself devoid of the effects you've just noted.
- See how your body and mind enter the bright purple light of the stone, eliminating the old energy patterns that supported your practice.

- Hold the amethyst using the left hand, use your ideal hand to light the paper over the candle flame. Leave it in a bowl to shake, as you say the following words:

"As I melt my energy with divine power, so do I. released from this trap; my life is now mine.

Mote it be."

- Put on your amulet properly and take three more deep breaths.
- Now, on the second piece of paper, compose a list of the positive results that leaving your habit or addiction

behind will bring into your life. Allow yourself to feel fired up and eager about these advantages of your newly found flexibility.

- When you're through, fold the paper three times and put it in front of the candle until the candle has burned all the way down.
- Keep the paper somewhere in your home (or carry it in your pocket or handbag) as a reminder of the positive manifestations you are now permitting into your life.
- Put the amethyst amulet in the pocket or wear it whenever you need energy assistance for remaining devoid of your old habit.

Bath Spell for Patience and Flexibility.

Using crystals in cleansing is a terrific way to produce a change in your energy field. If you discover yourself having a hard time with irritability and impatience, as we all do from time to time, this ritual bath can assist soothe those vibrations and restore you to a sense of peace and approval of life's little bumps in the roadway.

Adding necessary lavender oil to the relaxing energies of amethyst will increase the advantages of this bath; however, it's not strictly necessary.

You will require:

- One medium to large amethyst.
- White or purple candle.
- Lavender vital oil (optional).

Directions:

- Light the candle and run the bath.
- When the tub is midway full, include the lavender oil (if using).
- When you are bathing, ensure you are with your amethyst and take deep breaths gradually, and launching tension on the exhale. When the tub is filled, put the amethyst on the flooring of the tub near you and kick back and unwind.
- Wait in the bathing tub for about 15 minutes. Drain the bath when you are prepared.
- Remain in the tub as the water drains, so that any staying negative energy will be receded from your body and the amethyst.
- Gently extinguish the candle.
- Be sure to charge the amethyst and clean before using it in any other fantastic working.

Spell to Resolve Legal Issues.

If you discover yourself in legal difficulty, whether it's an overdue parking ticket or something more serious, staying calm is vital. Amethyst's ability to assist solve disputes and stop confrontational energies can help you find a resolution to your legal matters in a peaceful way. To prepare for this work, you may want to attempt the bath spell above.

(" Bath Spell for Patience and Flexibility") before you start.

You will require:

- One little amethyst crystal point.
- White candle.
- Two small muslin or other material squares.
- Needle.
- Blue thread.
- Orange thread.

Directions:

- Light the candle and take a couple of moments to quiet your mind.
- Insert the amethyst on top of one of the small material squares and put the other square on top of it.
- Beginning with the orange thread, sew the material squares together to confine the amethyst. As you sew,

display as factually as you can on the scenarios surrounding your legal concern.

- Use blue thread on your needle and stitch around the edges of the material again, this time concentrating your energy on clear communication, reality, and the peaceful resolution of your conflict.

- Put the appeal in front of a burning candle and state the following words:

" The powers of reality and reconciliation now infuse this wonderful development.".

- Permit the candle to stress out by itself.
- Place the amethyst in your pocket or bag when satisfying with an officer, attorney, or judge to help you focus your intent and bring about truthful and positive interaction.

Anti-Theft Travel Protection Spell

When checking out unknown places, specifically congested cities, it's always smart to keep a close eye on your belongings. You can likewise use a little bit of magic for some additional defense from those who would make the most of tourists.

This spell uses amethyst to protect you and your valuables from thieves so you can thoroughly enjoy your experiences. You can triple this spell or double as needed so that one charged amethyst is inside each of your luggage.

You will need:

- One amethyst per piece of travel luggage.
- Black spell candle.

Guidelines:

- Turn the candle on
- Place the amethyst on your hands and, merging your power to that of the Earth, conjure a sense of positive, protective energy.
- Focus this sensation unto the crystal.
- Watch the amethyst popping out a purple light serving as a protective glow from inside your suitcase (or knapsack).
- Expand the light so that it instills all of your items, then see it enveloping the entire travel box.
- When you believe the amethyst is wholly charged, then seal the energy by uttering the following words (or similar):.

" I pass through this world in peace and safety with all my personal belongings protect in my possession.

Let this be.".

- Keep the amethyst in front of the candle up until the candle has burned down.
- Then place it in your travel bag or sack throughout your journey.
- You can use that visualization to recharge the amethyst at any point throughout your journey if it feels required.

CHAPTER NINE

Citrine

This is another crystal typically found in magic and gemstone stores, this variety of quartz was called "citron" by the French just because of its similarity to a ripe lemon. Citrine is present in a variety of colors from pale yellow to dark amber, varying based on the amount of iron in the quartz crystal.

One traditional label for citrine is "the Sun Stone," due to its joyful color. Many citrine shine in the sunlight due to particles inside the stone, and the energy of this crystal is visibly positive, bringing the essence of sunshine in the form of joy, contentedness, and happiness. In reality, citrine has commonly been offered as presents to newborn babies for them to find a lifetime of emotional confidence and physical health.

Citrine was also called "the Merchant's Stone," understood to business people as a lucky talisman to be kept near the money register. A unique feature of citrine's wealth or commercial properties is that it not just assists you in obtaining wealth but also to maintain it. While other magical tools require the creation and build-up of riches, citrineenables the user to hang on to what they already have so it doesn't slip through their fingers.

Citrine'sconnection with the Planet Mercury as well as the element of Air, along with its yellow color, makes it an outstanding stone for magic having to do with concentration, visualization, decision-making as well as mental clarity in general. Communication issues and self-expression are also appropriate objectives when using this crystal. Anything needing a banishing of negativity and a boost in positive feelings can benefit from citrine, as this truly is a happy, uplifting stone.

In this chapter, you'll find out how to use citrine to energetically enhance the quality of your dreams, stay safe and secure in your finances, and rise above fear.

Cleansing Ritual with Citrine Stone

As with all of the standard magical tools, it's crucial to keep your crystals and other mineral stones clear of old, undesirable energies. There are lots of methods to clean your stones, but one basic approach is to use the purifying, fiery powers of citrine.

For excellent outcomes, clean raw and sleek stones independently, as jagged points or edges of natural stones might leave scratches in the polish. Make sure your citrine is charged and energetically clear before using it to clean your other stones.

The ritual is best done regularly, maybe once in a month on a bright day, or the eve of the Full Moon.

You will need:

- One medium to large piece citrine
- Large bowl
- Stones to be cleaned

Directions:

- Place the stones you would like to clean in the pan and place the citrine on top.

- Now, concentrating on your intention to clear unwanted energy, gently swirl the crystals together clockwise, using both hands.

- Repeat this twelve times to cleanse and get rid of unwanted energies present.

- After you have completed twelve swirls, remove the crystals from the bowl, and return the citrineright to your Altar.

- If you like, you may leave the cleansed stones out in the sun or moonlight for several hours to charge them with new natural energy.

Citrine Nightmare-Blasting Spell

For anyone who suffers from nightmares or undesirable dreams, citrine can work wonders. The brilliant energy of this crystal is like the Sun rupturing through the clouds, bring back color to the formerly grey landscape of your sleep. (In truth, you don't have to have "bad" dreams to gain from citrine-- try sleeping with a little piece under your pillow for a couple of nights and see if you don't see more pleasant, vivid adventures in your sleep!).

This spell uses citrine over the pineal eye, the spot above, and in between your seeing eyes that corresponds to your intuition. Integrating your intuition capabilities to clear stress from your body with the energies of citrine is an excellent way to enhance the quality of your dream experience.

This spell is most reliable when used before bedtime.

You will require:.

- One small piece of citrine.
- Fabric headband.

Directions:

- Put the citrine over your third eye and support it with the headband. Then lie on your back and take three deep breaths, focusing only on breathing in and breathing out.

Keep moving up through your body one part at a time--calves, thighs, hips, bowels, stomach, chest, hands, lower arms, shoulders, neck, and face. Simply acknowledge any form of tension you feel in any of those parts of your body—do not make any judgments or worry about them. Just be a neutral observer of the energy existing in your body.

- Now envision an intense, pleasant yellow light moving and getting in from the soles of your feet. See it taking a trip up throughout your body, wiping out any stress you found during the very first part of the cleaning procedure. Take the necessary time you need to make this visualization reliable, and repeat it as many times as you wish.
- When you feel relaxed, you can get rid of the citrine from your third eye and place it under your pillow.

- Have a deep sleep, and enjoy much better dreams than you have had in ages!

Citrine Spell for Maintaining Wealth

The ancient people of every culture saw the Sun as the source of abundance and prosperity, which might be relied on at the beginning of each new day. Citrine's association with the Sun makes it an excellent agent of security and long-term abundance.

When you work this easy spell, you declare your appreciation for what you already have, in addition to your receptivity to more wealth to come.

You will require:.

- One little piece of citrine.
- One dollar bill.
- Green or black ribbon or thick thread.
- Small drawstring bag.
- Work candles for the environment (optional).

Directions:

- Light the candle.

- Hold the citrineappropriately in your dominant hand and the dollar bill in your second hand.

- Take a deep breath as you focus your energy on merging the power of the citrine with the dollar bill and the yellow light, which signifies your current level of wealth.

- Then, wrap the dollar bill firmly around the citrine.

- Next step is to secure the dollar bill with the ribbon or thread, while chanting the following (or comparable) words until you have put it tightly in the right place:

" I hereby open the path to great wealth without any end."

- Put the wrapped citrine in the drawstring bag and keep it near your safe, checkbook, fireplace, or somewhere else in your house that symbolizes wealth.

Spell for Transmuting Fear

Many people have to wrestle with fear at one time or another--even Witches with the power of magic at their disposal. Whether you're facing a terrible monetary or health catastrophe, having to conquer a fear like the fear of flying, or fear for somebody else you care about, there's a limitation to the usefulness of fear.

Fear is only significant for prompting us to run out of burning buildings or preventing strolling alone during the night in harmful locations. To put it mildly, fear helps support sound judgment. Beyond that, and specifically in situations we can't manage, anxiety just disrupts clear thinking and informed decision making. This spell is used to transmute the energy of fear from your energy field by grounding it into the Earth, restoring you to calmness, and the capability to trust in the Universe.

Obviously, not all worry has an apparent source, and it's not uncommon for individuals to be living their lives while stunted by a more generalized fearful sensation. This is especially real for those who are bombarded by adverts, news stories, and other media that broadcast afraid messages daily.

Attempt adding a freewriting session to this spell if you discover that you are being fearful but can't recognize the cause. You can seek help from the Universe in finding whether there's something buried in your subconscious, whether you're merely getting the fearful energies of the dominant culture at large without understanding it.

This spell is preferably applied with raw citrine, rather than polished so that there's absolutely nothing in between the surface area of the stone and the Earth when you bury it. If you only have polished citrine, do not let that stop you!

You will require:

- One piece of citrine.
- White candle.
- Spade or little shovel.
- Journal or composing paper (optional).

Directions:

- Light the candle.
- If you include the composing component, invest 10 to 15 minutes composing about the fearful sensations you're planning to transmute.
- When you've reached a satisfying response to the question "what am I afraid of?", then you're all set to proceed to the next important step.
- Having the citrine between your palms, close your eyes, and take three deep breaths.
- Now, speak your fears into the stone. You can state them as loudly or as silently as you wish-- whatever makes you feel comfortable, however, you do require to speak (or whisper) out loud.
- Gently extinguish the candle as soon as you have released your fears into the citrine.

- Use the shovel or spade to bury the citrine outside, allowing the Earth to absorb your fear energy and transmute it to neutral voltage.
- Thank the Earth for getting involved with you in this work.
- For best results, do this action instantly after extinguishing the candle.

CHAPTER TEN

Moonstone

Moonstone is most likely one of the most captivating beautiful stones in any Wiccan's collection. The most significant deposits of moonstone are found mainly in Sri Lanka and India but found in other parts of the world

Moonstone was highly regarded in ancient Rome, where individuals wore the stone in numerous forms of precious jewelry. The ancient Egyptians likewise revered the moonstone, relating it with the goddess known as 'Isis.'

As a significant member of the feldspar family, moonstone is abundant, but the gorgeous specimens are ending up being a growing number of uncommon due to high demand. Moonstone ended up being extremely popular throughout the Art Nouveau duration, where it was included in a plethora of fashion jewelry pieces, and men even used moonstone in their cufflinks and view chains.

In recent times, the mineral has seen a resurgence of appeal in the fashion jewelry world, which may put the most sparkling pieces out of reach for a number of the amazingly inclined. However, you don't need to have the most lovely moonstone to work with its powerful magical energies!

The Moonstone's planetary association, with Water as its essential Element. So, this makes it a great stone to work within any spell related to tranquility, or feminine intuition, as well as any ritual honoring the Goddess. Fertility magic is a natural opportunity for using moonstone, as is any working related to women's reproductive health, renewing romantic enthusiasm, and increasing psychic receptivity.

Traditionally, moonstone was also used for security and safety while traveling at sea. In this regard, you'll find a spell below that is useful for having safe travel on or over water, in addition to periods to support efforts to develop a child, stimulate a long-term relationship, and motivate prophetic dreaming.

Water Travel Protection Spell

Travel by sea is not as frequent as it was centuries back when the custom of getting in touch with moonstone for safe passage over water would have been commonly practiced. Nonetheless, moonstone's watery energy is ideal for a modern-day variation of invoking travel defense, whether you're headed to the beach, going on a cruise, flying overseas, or going along a river.

Mugwort's association with the Moon makes it a perfect herb to accompany the moonstone for protection. If you are unable to find mugwort, you can replace it with another security herb, such as the bay leaf or valerian.

You will need:

- Three small moonstones
- One teaspoon fresh or dried mugwort
- Little drawstring bag
- Work candles for the environment (optional).

Instructions:

- Light the candle, if using.
- Hold the moonstones between your palms and envision the beams of the Moon getting in each stone. See the white rays of light coming in contact with the rocks and charging them with the use of protective energy that will develop a magical guard around you through your journey over water.
- Put the charged stones in the drawstring bag, and sprinkle the mugwort over them while saying the following (or comparable) words:

"As the Moon casts a glowing course across the sea, I will now surround me the energies of defense will.".

- Shut the drawstring bag and leave it under moonlight overnight, either outdoors or in a windowsill.
- Go along with it for extra safety on your travels.

Spell For Enhancing Fertility.

Deciding to bring a new soul into existence can be exciting and somewhat tricky for a couple. Sometimes, making a baby does not occur instantly, and each passing month might bring about a new level of frustration. The resulting stress and anxiety can negatively affect fertility.

Moonstone is a useful, excellent ally when you are ready to become a parent. This easy, however effective spell can relieve any fear about the ability to conceive and therefore boost fertility. As a bonus offer, moonstone is associated with the defense of women during pregnancy also.

You will require:

- One little piece moonstone.
- Needle and thread.
- Tee shirt or other often-worn product of clothing.
- Small square of green fabric.

Instructions:.

- Center yourself in the moment by positioning the moonstone in your hands and breathing deeply.
- Visualize your intent streaming into the stone.

- See yourself as a mother and father, inviting a new life into the world.
- Turn the shirt or other item of clothes inside out and place the moonstone in an area that won't get in your method when you wear it when you're prepared.
- Place the green square of material over it and stitch it onto the clothing. As you sew around the edges, consider the moonstone pouch as a womb for your intents to develop a kid.
- When you have entirely encased the stone in the garment, spend a minute holding it in your hands and state the following (or comparable) words:

"I invite you, a new kid of mine, into this life."

  - Place on the clothes and use it for the staying part of the day. Leave the stone in your unique pouch and wear the clothing frequently.
  - You can eliminate or take out the pouch and sew the fabric firmly when you've conceived over the stone to make it into a keepsake for your new child.

Moonstone Spell for Rekindling Passion.

Every relationship needs a boost of renewed passion at one point or another. Attempt working with captivated jewelry to breathe brand-new life into your present love regimen if you find yourself getting in a less-than-passionate stage with your partner. This working is best executed under a waxing or full moonlight.

You will require:.

- One moonstone locket.
- Red candle.

Directions:

- Light the candle.
- Hold the moonstone locket in your hands and take a moment to keep in mind times when you felt enthusiastic about your partner, and times when your partner demonstrated the same sensations towards you.
- Picture a new encounter with your partner that revives the energies. If you find just a single stone in the necklace, focus more on holding that single stone as you think about the past and future enthusiasm in your relationship.
- Repeat the process with each one if the pendant has more than one moonstone.
- When you have totally charged your locket with passionate energies, put it on, close your eyes, breathe deeply, and enable yourself to take pleasure in anticipation of manifesting your desires on the real airplane.
- Gently extinguish the candle.

- Use the locket on your next date or other quality time with your partner.

Moonstone Dreaming Spell.

When we're living hectic, busy lives, our dreams can often look like merely a string of ridiculous "brain garbage" that don't cause much in the way of insight. However, typically, dreaming is suggested to be an automobile for essential messages from deep space and our more fabulous selves.

There are lots of crystals that can help clear out the mess of our subconscious and smooth out the course to help us have more profound, more lucid, and even prophetic dreams. Moonstone happens to be one of the most powerful stones for dreaming, as its energies are connected with the shifting, psychic tides of the Moon.

The spell calls for surrounding yourself with moonstone, producing an energy grid that will help you link to the heavenly plane in your sleep. You can take it an action even more if you like, asking for specific guidance to come to you in your dreams on the night you work the spell.

You will require:.

- Four small moonstones.
- Silver candle.

- Journal or composing paper.

Directions:

- Light the candle and spend a couple of minutes silencing your mind.
- If you have any particular challenge or problem that you would like to have resolved in the dream, write it on a sheet of paper (at the top).
- Hold the moonstones purposefully in your hands and visualize your personal energy instilling them up until they radiance. Quietly ask the stones to harness the power you require to receive dreams that include beneficial details.
- Now, keep one piece of moonstone on the floor at each corner of your bed. As you put each stone, state the following words (or something similar):

" By the light emerging from the Moon, my dreams will stream and tell me all I need to understand. So be it."

- Gently snuff out the candle before going to sleep.

- Keep the journal or composing paper (and pen) near your bed so that you can record your dreams very first thing after waking.

CHAPTER ELEVEN

Carnelian

Carnelian is a range of chalcedony quartz, colored with reds, oranges, ambers, and browns by impurities of iron oxide. Its dynamic colors look like that of a sunset, which made it the description "sunset confined in stone" in the old Egypt.

Take care if buying online; however, as some carnelian stones are agates, which have been heated and dyed.

Found mostly in India but also in South America and Madagascar, this stone has been used for countless years to safeguard against evil energies. It was made use of by the ancient Egyptians as a sign of the goddess Isis to secure against anger, jealousy, and malice, in addition to for renewal and vigor. Therapists throughout these times used carnelian to aid with blood problems. This stone was likewise part of ancient Eastern burial routines, frequently accompanying the dead as a protective talisman.

A stone fittingly connected with the Sun and the Element of Fire, carnelian can be used to boost one's nerve and express one's individuality without aggression. Speaker, stars, and entertainers of all kinds can benefit from its energy, as suggested by two standard labels for carnelian: "the Actor's Stone" and "the Singer's Stone."

Nevertheless, you need not be "natural" on phase to take advantage of the confidence- giving powers of this stone, anybody finding themselves having to provide a discussion or speech can contact the carnelian to help them succeed, no matter just how much they might fear the job.

Carnelian is one of the high protection spells, for as sunshine clears away shadows, this stone's energy eradicates negativity. Below, you will find spells for protecting versus negative energies, motivating positive self-expression, enhancing creative energy, and honing focus and concentration.

Empath's Spell for Banishing Harmful Energy

In the grand plan of things, being an empath is a blessing and a present. Still, it can likewise be a threat, as ultra-sensitive types can get slowed down, depressed, nervous, and even physically ill from too much exposure to lower vibrational, harmful energies. Whether it's due to staying in a hazardous workplace day, being the subject of another person's angry or hostile thoughts, or merely being in a physical space where past catastrophes have occurred, it's not unusual for Wiccans and other beautiful people to end up being adversely impacted by the type of energy around them.

The bold power of the carnelian makes it an outstanding stone of security against the negative impacts of all kinds. To increase the overall result of the spell, try taking a ritual cleaning bath and smearing yourself with sage, lavender, or other purifying herbs before you begin.

You will require:

- One piece of carnelian
- Small bell or chime
- Black candle

Directions:

- Light up the black candle and then sit in a comfortable chair with your feet flat on the ground.
- Holding the carnelian in between your palms, take a moment to concentrate on your physique and set a desire for clearing up your energy field.
- Put the carnelian properly on the floor close to your feet. Beginning with the soles of your feet, visualize any negativeness surrounding your feet and ankles being absorbed by the carnelian stone. (This energy might take the kind of dark, wispy, smoke like-tendrils in your mind's eye.).
- Next, position the carnelian in your lap. Imagine it cleaning your calves, thighs, and hip area in the same way.
- Bring the carnelian close to your chest to clear the upper torso and repeat the visualization.
- Place it near your throat to clean your shoulders and neck area.

- Finally, position the carnelian on the top of your head to cleanse your whole self and your surrounding aura.
- When you're completed, thank the stone and put it in front of the candle. Sounding the bell or chime over the sand to clear and recharge its energy, then gently extinguish the black candle.
- Place the stone in a location where you will stroll past it numerous times a day, so you can be reminded that you are protected from any unwanted energy.

Self-confidence Speaking Spell for Introverts.

Lots of people who are quite articulate in a one-on-one setting discover themselves unwilling to speak in group scenarios, whether it's a college class, a conference at work, or perhaps a social night out.

If this describes your personality, try bringing this simple appeal with you the next time you're communicating with others. You just might be shocked by the difference it makes!

You will require:

- One little piece of carnelian.
- Yellow, orange, or white candle.

Instructions:.

- Light the candle and spend a long time quieting your mind.
- Think of a recent period when you had something to contribute to a conversation, but kept it to yourself rather than sharing.
- Now pick up the carnelian and envision the scene once again; however, this time, see yourself stating what you desired to say. See the energy of your declaration spreading out light like a beacon throughout the environment of the scene.
- While still having a hold on the stone, repeat the following statement (or something similar)nine times:

" My voice has strong value, and other people will hear me."

- If you wish, think of another scene to "reword" in this way, and after that, repeat the statement nine more times. Then, continue this process until you feel a shift of confidence in your energy.
- Bring the carnelian with you next time you are in a group setting and watch as you begin to communicate your thoughts and ideas with confidence.

Spell to Spark Creativity.

Whether you're a writer handling author's block, an artist suffering from a lack of new ideas, or just wanting to shake things up a little in any innovative area of your life, this ritual is exceptional for reconnecting with your individual "muse." It's likewise excellent for merely unwinding and carrying yourself out of the everyday grind and into playful, magical co-creation with deep space.

The carnelian energy on your paper as you allow your right-brained consciousness to stream makes this crystal an actual "touchstone" linking you to the more magnificent worlds of creative manifestation.

Keep in mind: this spell has absolutely nothing whatsoever to do with artistic talent, so do not be intimidated if you're not the "artist" type. If you're someone who is always stating things like "I'm not artistic" or "I'm not truly imaginative," then you need to work this spell as often as possible!

You will require:

- One-piece carnelian Orange candle
- White paper.
- Markers, crayons, paints, or drawing pencils.
- Music (optional).

Guidelines:.

- Light up the candle and put on some music that motivates you in some method, if you wish.
- Place the paper and drawing/painting on the altar or table in front of you.
- Keep the carnelian stone anywhere on the paper.
- Just allow your drawing tool to swirl and move throughout the page freely, without thought or concern for producing a gorgeous piece of art. No one will see your development (unless you want them to).

- Carefully snuff out the candle when you feel that you are done.

- You can place your piece of launched creativity on your altar, ultimately view, fold it up and put it someplace discreet, and even get rid of it if you wish.

- Repeat this ritual whenever you need to spark a creative burst of energy for a task, or simply wish to participate in magical have fun with the Universe.

Spell for Beginning a Long-Term Project.

Whether you're composing a term paper, assembling a presentation, or even preparing to move home, it can be simple to get lost in the details of a big, multifaceted job. This basic spell helps you stay grounded and focused as you move through the different phases of your career.

If you haven't currently, take the first few minutes of the spell to make a list of the specific jobs that comprise your general task, taking this step will help you decrease any feelings of overwhelm, even before you finish the spell.

You will need:.

- One-piece carnelian.
- Orange ribbon or thick thread.
- One piece of writing paper (optional).
- Many post-it notes or small squares of paper.
- Work candle for atmosphere (optional).

Directions:

- Light the candle, if using. Invest some time quieting your mind, and after that create the "to do" list discussed above, either on paper or mentally.

- Now, jot down one task per post-it note, developing a stack of specific, workable jobs that will amount to the completed job.

- Put them in the order of what to be done first, second, third, and so on (without getting too hung up on private information, as you wish to be able to be versatile)
- Place the carnelian in between your palms, close your eyes, and spend a couple of moments envisioning the completed job. How will you feel when you're finished?

- When you have developed a stable, confident feeling about finishing the task, open your eyes, and state the words below (or something similar):.

" Step by step, one after the other, these tasks of mine will soon be done. So be it.".

- Place the carnelian right on top of the stack of notes, and put the pile on your desk or some other location where you will see it frequently while you work.

- As you total each task, take the corresponding note from the stack under the carnelian and tear it up into pieces.
- Take pleasure in enjoying the stack grow smaller sized and take convenience in the energies of the carnelian, assisting you in pushing on to the next action.

CHAPTER TWELVE

Bloodstone

Its common name would appear to suggest a mainly red coloring; bloodstone is, in fact, a deep green form of jasper with flecks of red and brown caused by iron oxide pollutants in the stone. The name "bloodstone" comes from Christian folklore, which holds that the blood from the crucifixion of Jesus spattered onto the green jasper stones below the cross. This mineral was also called "heliotrope" to the ancient Greeks, which translates approximately to "sunstone."

For many years, bloodstone has been used by various cultures to recover and ground the body through its purification and detoxification homes. The ancient Mésopotamiensusually dipped the stones in cold water and applied them to the skin over essential organs for detoxification. Also, Bloodstone was ground to a powder form and mixed with honey to draw out snake venom after a bite.

As a well-rounded promoter of vibrant physical health, bloodstone was believed to have the ability to reduce or stop bleeding arising from injuries. Perhaps this is the reason why warriors wore the stone for an additional increase of courage and protection throughout the battle.

Aligned with the planet Mars and the component of Fire, bloodstone supports spells focused around resolving negativeness and can be used to bring positive energy into any scenario. Indeed, as a green stone, it can continuously be included in cash spells for an additional increase, and it has also been used in magic associated with weather.

The spells below use the residential or commercial properties of bloodstones to assist one to recognize and avoid deception, strengthen relationships between kids and mothers, gain defense from bullies, and make difficult choices.

Bloodstone Deception Detection Spell

This spell works in scenarios where you're unsure you can trust what you're being told, whether it's at work, a social gathering, or perhaps within a relationship. Bloodstone resolves negativity and opens up access to personal assistance, while the color blue is related to genuineness, truth, and fidelity. As you carry this bloodstone beauty with you, it will continue to assist you in seeing the fact more clearly and accurately.

You will need:

- Blue spell candle
- Blue thread
- One small piece bloodstone
- Small square of a blue fabric

Instructions:

- Light up the candle.
- Place bloodstone right on top of the blue material on your altar or table.

- Place both of your hands right above the stone and focus on surrounding the stone with the dark blue light of fact.
- When it seems you have filled the stone with your energetic light, repeat the following (or similar) words three times:

"I distinguish between reality and untruth. I am secured from deceptiveness."

- Wrap the bloodstone thoroughly in the material, secure it with the blue thread, and place it in front of the candle.
- Allow the candle to stress out by itself.
- Take the charmed stone with you in your pocket or purse to help secure yourself from all forms of deception.
- You may also hold it in your hand or while in your pocket during discussions to feel whether or not you are being tricked.

- Charge it with the above routine whenever you feel the requirement.

Spell to Strengthen The Mother and Child Relationships

The bond existing between a mother and her child is profound and spiritual; however that does not imply that conflict between the two will not take place periodically (or frequently!), particularly at certain phases in life. This spell assists in strengthening the loving energy between mother and kid, and the gift can be given as a method of calming an existing dispute or avoiding a future one.

Bloodstone is related to motherhood, which makes it an exceptional focal point for this beautiful working; however, you can replace another crystal if you wish.

Considering that this is a present rather than a beauty you use yourself, it's essential to be mindful of your intentions here. This working is not about controlling the ideas or behaviors of another person, but about fostering caring energy between 2 individuals. The difference is essential, so if you're in genuinely hostile conflict with your mom and are not able to summon calm, caring sensations, then this is not an excellent spell for you to operate at this time.

You will need:

- Bloodstone precious jewelry (such as a ring, bracelet, pendant, and so on)
- Pink candle

Directions:

- Place the bloodstone fashion jewelry on the table or altar in front of you and light the candle.
- Hold the precious jewelry carefully between your palms.
- Then, visualize yourself with your mother (or anyone else to whom you want to strengthen a bond with). See yourself communicating in a calm and tranquil way.
- Visualize yourself taking a deep breath when you feel your feelings increasing, or politely excusing yourself to be able to take a minute to soothe yourself before returning to the conversation.
- After the visualization, infuse the necklace with relaxing energy as you state the following (or similar) words:

"As above, so below

Our relationship continues to grow.

As below, so above

Our communication is filled with love

So be it."

- Provide the charmed jewelry as a present for a birthday or holiday or as an "even if" present.

Anti-Bullying Protection Spell

When facing their challenger, warriors of the past were known to wear a bloodstone amulet close to their hearts to provide the courage. The red specks of intense Mars energy integrated with the deep Earthy green hues imbue a feeling of well-fortified security. This protective amulet can protect you from if you're in the regrettable scenario of dealing with somebody who acts in a bullying way towards you their negativeness. You'll quickly be well out of their radar and left alone because bullies only target individuals they believe they can have a result on. This protective magic at its finest!

If you do not have a pendant including bloodstone, you can make one by wrapping the wire around the stone and connecting it to any kind of pendant cord You can also find simple cables with small wire "baskets" that permit you to put crystals of your choice inside them, successfully serving as an all-purpose crystal pendant.

You will need:

- One bloodstone locket or pendant
- Black spell candle

Instructions:

- Light the candle.
- In a sitting position, place the locket or pendant in your lap.

- Begin by envisioning a beautiful green orb sitting in the middle of your lap. See the sphere grow gradually as it envelops you within it. This is your unusual force- field, protecting you versus your opponent.
- On the external edge of this shielding energy, picture dynamic spots of red flaring up to caution away anyone who would do your damage.
- When you've summoned a peaceful, protected sensation, hold the bloodstone within your palms and say the following words (or something similar):

"I am secured from all who mean me damage, with the Heart of Earth and the Fire of Mars,

This amulet guards me against their gaze and sends them on their method. Let it be."

- Place the amulet right in front of the candle and permit the candle to burn out on its own.
- Use it around your neck whenever you might come into contact with those who would bully you.

Bloodstone Divination for Big Decisions

When you're facing a primary choice in life with lots of possible options, it can be challenging to get a clear answer from your instinct alone. During this spell, you will evaluate all of the possible outcomes of a decision and enable this beautiful stone to assist you in choosing which course to sail.

You will require:

- One small to medium piece of bloodstone.
- One blank and unlined sheet of paper.
- Pen or Black marker

Directions:

- Take some deep breaths and reflect quietly on the choice you have before you.
- Place the bloodstone in the middle of the paper.
- With the pen or marker, draw the line radiating outside from the stone for every one of your possible options. The edges should be separated at least an inch apart.
- Now take out the stone and hold it correctly in your hand.
- Next, close your eyes, take a long, deep breath, and then roll or drop the stone in the middle of the paper, bearing in mind where it lands.
- The line's closest to (or straight on) the option you're being asked to think about.
- Inspect with your gut; you will get a definite yes or no on this specific option. Repeat the procedure as required until the final choice is clear

CHAPTER THIRTEEN

Jade

The stone we refer to as jade involves two different minerals that have extremely comparable residential or commercial properties. Jade has been used in many cultures for making a variety of items varying from ax heads to incense burners to fashion jewelry.

Jade is among the most revered stones of magic; numerous traditions have honored its powers from a long time to the present moment. Holding the stone firmly in the palm of their ideal hands, ancient traders would count on its capabilities to make the most effective possible choice throughout business transactions. In China, jade has long been thought to harness and hold the power of all five of the Chinese virtues of humanity: benevolence, knowledge, righteousness, propriety, and fidelity. You can observe symbols of all five of the attributes sculpted into jade stones throughout China.

The Mayans and Aztecs also carved pictures of their deities out of Jade and used it for its medicinal qualities. Known across the world as a stone aligned with the bladder and kidney, Jade has been called by many unique names, such as the spleen stone, yu stone, stone of the loin, piedra de hijada, as well as the stone of flank. In recent times, people take Jade to support the immune system throughout times of tension.

Jade is also aligned with Element of Water, the planet Neptune and its restorative energy supply relaxing vibrations that cover the user in a shield of protective energy. Jade promotes knowledge, balance, and peace and is particularly helpful during difficult times in life. This stone can help clear out old psychological patterns to bring clearness to a complicated scenario. Some of the magical uses for Jade include security, new love, abundance, gardening, and dream work. The spells below use Jade to promote balance and prosperity, assist with fast decision making, and deal with the feelings of guilt.

A Spell to Restore Balance

Typically, when we hear the word "stress," it raises unfavorable connotations. This is mostly as a result of the imbalances of mainstream modern life, where busyness rule the day, and the value of associating with the Earth and the spiritual realm is forgotten. Though, stress does have beneficial qualities in moderate quantities, as it helps us recognize when we are overworked, out of balance, or perhaps in some form of danger.

The Chinese symbol known as yin and yang represents the interconnectedness of all things and the balancing of opposites. This visual symbol of darkness within light and lightness within dark reveals to us that our Universe is made up of seemingly opposite yet complementary qualities, such as stress and ease, forcefulness, and patience, as well as gentleness and firmness.

This spell will help you bring back the balance within you, and works for times when you feel excessively stressed, irritable, or anxious.

You will need:

- Two pieces of jade.
- Yin-yang symbol (drawn or printed).

Directions:

- Place the yin-yang sign on the altar or table in front of you. Put one piece of Jade on either side of the image.

- Invest some time silencing your mind as you keep a mild focus on the symbol.

- Using your left hand, pick up the jade to the right of the symbol and hold it tight. Using your right hand, move up the Jade to the left and hold it so fast.

- Hold one closed palm across the white circle within the black half of the yin- yang, and the other across the black ring in the half of the white.

- Have three deep breaths in this place, and envision the power of the yin- yang paired with the energies of the jade stabilizing any anxiousness in your life. Consider any elements of your life that need more balance and ask the Universe to assist you in restoring equilibrium to those areas.

- Place the stones straight on the yin-yang sign when you are through with your contemplation.
- It's either you leave them on your altar or in another prominent place until you ascertain your balance has been brought back.

Spell for Prosperous Beginnings

Whether you're beginning a business, moving into a new house, starting a new task, or inviting a new member into your household, milestones like these are exceptional events for a little magic.

The scarab beetle was thought to be a sign of prosperity and rejuvenation in ancient cultures ranging from Egypt to China. As a magical sign, it's an appropriate counterpart to Jade, which is highly valued as a success stone in the conventional Chinese system of Feng Shui.

You will need:

- Three small to medium pieces of Jade.
- Green spell candle.
- Potted plant.
- Image of a scarab.

Directions:

- Put the scarab image on the table or altar before you.
- Assemble the jade stones in a triangle around the scarab, and put the candle near the top rock.
- Light the candle and profess the words below (or similar):

" My success, luck, fortune accompany me on this new important journey.".

- Allow the candle to stress out itself.
- Bury the Jade around the potted plant and embellish the pot with the picture of the scarab.
- Place the plant in a prominent place where you will be constantly reminded of its thriving energy and the fantastic potential of the new beginning you are commemorating.

Spell for Resolving Feelings of Guilt.

Everyone feels guilt over a particular situation at some point in their lives. In some cases, this is because of the choices we've made that caused harm to another, but we might also have feelings of guilt even though we're not at fault. Whether it arises from misplaced blame or real wrongdoing, regret is a negative emotion that can sap us of happiness, essential wellness, and excellent health.

This spell will help you find the nerve to make apologies and reparations if suitable, or just enable you to move on and release the regret or guilt in your life. Because you will be put in the ground the jade, simple pieces are perfect, but you may still use refined jade if need be.

You will need:

- One or more pieces of raw jade
- Spade.
- Light blue spell candle
- Journal or writing paper (which is optional).

Directions:

- Light the candle and spend a few minutes contemplating the source(s) of your guilty feelings or feelings of regret. You may wish to write about it to get a clearer understanding of your role in a particular situation.
- Choose a jade stone and put it on your dominant palm when you're ready.
- Envision the situation, which has caused you to feel guilt.
- Close your eyes, and permit the jade to soak up this memory.
- Now, picture yourself making an apology, if required, and making any necessary reparations to correct the situation. Take the recovery energy of this pictured scenario and see it as a white light pouring into the palm of your non-dominant hand.
- Position your non-dominant hand over the jade. Depending on the intricacy of the situation you are working to heal, you may desire to repeat this procedure with additional jade stones.

- When you complete the ritual, bury the stone(s) in the Earth to let go of the formal feelings of guiltiness.

- If you need to apologize and amends to others, do so promptly to heal from the experience fully.

Split-Second Decision Spell

As a supporter of wisdom and clarity in fast-moving circumstances, jade is ideal for scenarios needing quick choices under pressure, whether on the task or in other areas of your life. One charged stone in your pocket or handbag can help you make every call with self-confidence.

You will need:.

- One medium piece jade.

Instructions:

- Grip the jade between your palms and take a deep breaths.
- Close your eyes and see yourself covered in quiet, peaceful energy. In this state, you can quickly access your personal assistance.
- Call a feeling of self-confidence and self-trust as you envision yourself making fast, accurate decisions that will have lasting positive results on the people.
- When you are ready, send this energy of calm self-esteem into the stone, and then state the following (or comparable) words:

  " As rapidly as I touch this stone, all I need for my choice is understood. So let it be.".

- Bring the jade with you in situations where you encounter the need to make decisions rapidly.

CHAPTER FOURTEEN

Malachite

It's groups of much lighter stones, and deep emerald greens creating a striking look, and its relative softness makes it a famous stone for sculpting into distinct shapes. This copper carbonite mineral was called by the ancient Greeks after the leaves of the mallow plant (or "Malachi" in Greek).

Malachite was mined in the Sinai area of Egypt since 4000 BCE. Related with wealth and travel, this was a well-known stone with ancient traders and merchants. Traders would use the stone while conducting a group in order to enhance the success of their deals. Merchants would keep malachite with their cash to increase their financial holdings. In many regions, malachite became called "the salesperson's stone." It was as well known for its protective nature, nevertheless, and was worn in some areas of Italy to ward off the wicked eye.

Among different ways, malachite has been used throughout the ages is purification. The intense green of the malachite stone absorbs negativeness and toxins from the body and the environment around us. The toxic substances of the earth, such as radiation, and the contaminants of the body, such as stomach pains, can both be extracted using the heavenly powers of malachite. Ironically, however, malachite is poisonous to the human body and must never be taken in an elixir or consumed in any form. To be on the safe side, deal with sleek malachite rather than its raw form.

Related to the world of Venus and the Element of Earth, the protective residential or commercial properties of malachite are quite strong. When there is an impending threat or splinter to alert of negative energies, the stone has been known to break. Malachite likewise helps to ward off headaches and diseases and is an especially excellent security stone for kids.

As a stone of improvement, it is used magically to help change psychological, physical, or spiritual circumstances from negative to favorable by removing the adverse energies. Wearing malachite on the skin helps attract love and make the user more ready to let love into their life.

Malachite is used in beautiful workings related to love, money, travel, defense, and boosting psychic abilities. It is stated that the stone will improve the incredible power of spellwork or prophecy. The spells listed below make use of malachite to safeguard sleeping children, lower road rage, calm fears of flying,

fend off unwanted electronic communications.

Roadway Rage Reduction Spell

For those who handle congested commutes to and from work, traffic can damage a favorable attitude. The people that know the Law of Attraction understand that getting frustrated tends to lead to even more discouraging circumstances!

This enjoyable little spell makes use of malachite's ability to reduce the effects of unfavorable circumstances to assist you in remaining calm, relaxed, and collected in any traffic scenario, leaving your ability to attract real situations undamaged.

You will require:

- One small malachite stone
- Small toy cars and truck
- White or yellow spell candle

Instructions:

- Place the malachite and the small toy automobile in the middle of your altar or workspace.

- Get the stone and hold it in your dominant hand.

- Close your eyes and imagine yourself in your automobile on the open road. Permit yourself to feel the ease, pleasure, and liberty of taking a trip quickly and smoothly to your location.

- Take a couple of deep breaths as you allow this favorable vibrational frequency to take hold in your consciousness. Visualize the energy of this sensation, instilling the malachite with you.

- When you notice the stone is fully charged, put the stone on top of the toy car.

- Now, picture yourself stuck in traffic. As you discover the feelings of stress and anxiety and frustration start to appear, select up the malachite and allow the energy, you just charged it with to diffuse the negativity you've simply conjured. Keep in mind the difference in how you feel after holding the stone for sometimes.

- Return the stone on top of the car and light the candle as you say the following (or comparable) words:

"As the speed of traffic stops and begins

I remain centered in my heart.

No matter how the traffic's streaming

I always

ys get to where I'm going."

- Allow the candle to stress out itself.

- Keep the toy car in your glove section, and hold the malachite handy to keep whenever you wind up in heavy traffic.

Magical Malachite Message Minimizer

Since the advent of the "cell phone," the quantity of time we invest in dealing with texts, e-mails, and phone calls has more than quadrupled. (For those who likewise use social media, this interruption aspect is multiplied significantly!) All of this communication can result in a messy mind, making it harder to shift into a magical frame of mind at the end of the day.

The simplest solution is to leave the phone turned off, or silence informs for new messages when we desire a break, this isn't always possible. However, it is possible to reduce the "sound" related to undesirable, unnecessary contact with the cyber-world.

Contemporary techno-pagans have discovered that malachite works in safeguarding versus any unfavorable energies connected with our modern forms of communication. Use this spell to assist you in defending against the minor (or major) disruptions that undesirable e-mails, texts, and calls can trigger in the circulation of your everyday life.

Note that your intention ought to be focused on eliminating undesirable communication so that only people you want to communicate with will contact you.

You will need:

- One medium to sizeable malachite stone
- Phone (or computer system).

Guidelines:

- Put the malachite on your phone or computer.

- With your hand still touching the stone, imagine a shield of green light surrounding you and your gadget, avoiding any unwanted communications.

- See the grave green stone absorbing all unwanted, congested energy from your everyday interactions on this gadget and transmuting it into tranquil, quiet power.

- If you like, state the following (or comparable) words as you charge the stone with your power:

"Do not call, do not push 'send.' Unwanted messages now will end.

Let it be.".

- Leave the malachite on or near your gadget to continue to ward off unwanted interactions throughout the day.

Energy Protection Charm for Children.

Kids are little psychic sponges and are continuously detecting the moods and emotions of grownups, whether we understand it or not. Some kids are even more sensitive than others (particularly those who end up thinking about the magical arts!); however, all children are energetically susceptible to their surroundings to some degree.

Even the most loving moms and dads go through psychological struggles that can permeate into the subconsciousness of their children. This is all part of human advancement, but we can use magic to minimize the impacts our unfavorable energies have on the youths around us.

Malachite is traditionally referred to as a defense stone for kids. Making a malachite beauty to await your kid's room creates an invisible shield to keep out unwanted energies, entities, and anything else on the heavenly airplane that may cause unnecessary problems. It's perfect for hanging this beauty in a window so that it can charge daily in the sunlight. If this isn't possible, just make sure to charge the stone routinely, preferably in direct sunlight.

You will need:

- One small to medium piece malachite.
- 4 to 5 inches of thin wire.
- 8 to 12 inches of thick thread.
- Hook.
- Work candles for the environment (optional).

Guidelines:

- Light the candle, if in use.

- Spend some time calming your mind and breathing deeply. This is a particularly essential first step, provided the focus of this working, you don't desire any tension, worry, or other negative energy to be in your field as you charge this beauty and creativity.

- Hold one edge of the wire against the malachite and start covering the length around the stone.

- As you work, imagine the stone radiating favorable energy in the child's room and continuing over the window. See the power of the rock breaking through and dissipating any destructive power that could enter your child's unconscious mind.

- As an additional energetic increase, attempt singing or humming a lullaby while you protect the stone within the wire.

- Use the thread to make a wall mount for the stone with a loop.

- Put the hook on the window and hang the pendant in the sunlight (if possible), being mindful to hang it high adequate to be out of the reach of kids.

Spell to Soothe Fears of Flying.

Even in this modern-day age of frequent flight, the worry of flying is not unusual if this fear has kept you on the ground in the past, attempt using the protective, soothing energies of malachite to assist you to overcome your fear.

This spell includes getting in touch with the protective powers of a chosen divine being or other magical beings. If you deal with the God and Goddess, you can call on them directly for this spell, or discover an element of them amongst the ancient deities connected with journeys, such as Hermes, Apollo or Rhiannon. Additionally, you could request for the support of Archangel Raphael, who guards travelers. Call on the sylphs to keep you boosted and feeling safe during your flight if you work with the Elementals.

You will need:.

- Two small to medium malachite stones.
- Sheet of white paper.

Directions:

- Take three deep breaths and imagine a white light burning from your stones
- Allow the light to grow on each inhale up until you are covered in a soft white glow.

- Turn the white paper to make a paper airplane when you're prepared to begin. You can fold your airplane in any design that you like.
- Put one malachite stone on each of the wings. Focus your energy and intent on the aircraft as you let it represent your upcoming travel.
- Now imagine yourself being brought on the wings of your selected excellent assistant(s). Imagine them carrying you gently through the sky, knowing that you are safe and can relax on their sides.
- Spend a few minutes holding quickly to this vision, and then place the stones on your altar up until your next journey through the air. You can keep the paper plane on the platform or recycle it as well.
- Bring the enchanted malachite with you in your pocket or purse for your next flight.

During launch (and during the flight, if need be), hold the stones to recall the safe and peaceful feeling you had during your visualization. Silently ask your picked excellent assistant(s) to stick near to you throughout the flight.

CHAPTER FIFTEEN

Tiger's Eye

Tiger's Eye is known as a macrocrystalline quartz, consisted of numerous interwoven layers of earthy browns and glimmering gold hues. The resemblance of the stones to a tiger's fur, in addition to the appearance of "eyes" in most of the smooth stones, resulted in the name of this mineral. As symbols of animals, tigers represent power, strength, and sophistication, and these attributes are associated with the stone also.

The ancient Egyptians used the tiger's eye stones as real eyes in sculptures of their goddesses and gods, representing the ability of the divine to see all and know all. In the East, the tiger's eye has long been connected with wealth and good fortune. Ancient Roman soldiers wore and carried the stones in battle, as they believed it had the power to make weapons bounce off of their armor. More substantially, these amulets provided the user nerve to stand up to an enemy on the fight field and defend what he thought was right.

Tiger's eye is useful for focusing the mind, bringing about clarity, improving spiritual visions, and supporting the required transformation that should happen throughout the journey of life. Associated with the Sun and the Elements of Earth and Fire, this stone is likewise used in functions for defense from psychic attack, wealth and prosperity, and great fortune in new endeavors.

Some individuals use the tiger's eye's animal connection to work magic for the security and preservation of tigers and other huge cats, both in the wild and in refuge parks. In this chapter, you'll discover spells using the tiger's eye to bring success to a new business endeavor, look for clearness in a murky scenario, and provide yourself with a boost of guts and bravery, along with a creative divination ritual.

Spell for a Successful New Business

Beginning a new business is a massive leap of faith, even for the most skilled entrepreneurs. This spell assists you in getting off on the best foot, adding an object of personal importance to you with three main features or qualities of the tiger's eye: wealth, excellent fortune, and success. You'll be putting in place a talisman to aesthetically advise you of your future success throughout every day.

You will need:

- Some small tiger's eye stones
- Journal or composing paper
- Green or gold candle
- Small dish, bowl, or cup that has personal importance

Directions

- Light the candle and take a few deep breaths.
- Invest a long time considering what "success" in your business appears like. Perhaps it's a shop full of customers searching the merchandise, or a significant personnel of well-compensated employees. You might visualize numerous five-star evaluations on a social network site, or satisfied customers were referring your business to their friends.

- Do some conceptualizing along these lines and make a list of many manifestations of "success" as you can think of. Be as precise as you can with the provided details.

- Now hold some of the tiger's eye stones in your hand and make a loose fist. Close your eyes and picture one of the manifestations from your list, being as abundant in detail as you can.

- Place the stone in the cup, bowl, or dish.

- Repeat this procedure with the remainder of the stones--imagining your success and then putting the energy of it into the vessel.

- When you are done, find a particular area in your new company to put the vessel to ensure excellent fortune and success.

Refocusing Spell for Long-Term Projects

When dealing with long-term tasks such as academic papers or discussions, it's simple to get bogged down in the nitty-gritty information and lose focus, which makes it challenging to stay motivated. Even when taking a useful approach, such as beginning with the most favorable aspects and conserving the hardest parts for the future, there are overwhelming moments that can make finishing the work appear difficult.

In this spell, the tiger's eye represents the "all-seeing eye" that can view every angle of a situation. You will draw on its energies to rise above the information and see the project come together into a cohesive whole.

You will need:

- One medium to big tiger's eye stone
- One sheet of essential size yellow or blue paper
- Numerous small slips of paper

Directions:

- Place the tiger's eye in the center of the blue or yellow paper on your altar or work area.

- On every one of the sheets of paper, write a word or phrase that represents an angle of the task that you're battling with. These can be more significant concerns, such as meeting the task deadline, down to the smallest, most confounding information, such as how to rework a disorganized paragraph.

- As soon as you've written each issue on a sheet of paper, take a moment to focus your gaze on the tiger's eye. Imagine yourself taking a look at the task from a high vantage point and see it coming together as if being sewn with gold stitches by an unseen hand.

- Hold this vision for a few minutes and allow a sensation of self-confidence to develop within you.

- When you feel sufficiently definite about completing the job, collect all the sheets of paper and fold them into the yellow or blue paper.

- Place the tiger's eye on top of the folded paper and leave it on your table or altar up until you have completed the job.

Tiger's Eye Courage Spell

Tiger's eye empowered even the strongest Roman soldiers to be brave and bold during a fight. Just as the soldiers used the tiger's eye to deflect weapons wielded by the people attacking them, we can use the tiger's eye to deflect fear triggered by challenging social scenarios.

This spell will enable you to produce a metaphorical guard to bring with you into whatever battles you face, whether they involve having a hard conversation with your boss, dealing with daunting colleagues, or perhaps a vacation dinner with sone of your in-laws.

You will need:

- Four pieces of tiger's eye
- Little cloth bag
- Red spell candle

Directions:

- Take a couple of deep breaths and make yourself comfortable.

- Envision the approaching encounter you're concerned about. See yourself in the moment after the meeting has come to a close, feeling satisfied and relieved with the way you handled the circumstance. You don't have to visualize any of the details-- simply focus on the feeling of having successfully dealt with the challenge.

- When you're all set, light the candle. Place the very first stone in front of the candle and state the following words (or something similar):

  " I honor myself for acknowledging my worries."

- Place the second stone behind the candle, straight in line with the very first, and say the following (or similar) words:
  " I trust my intuition to direct my words."

- Place the third stone to the right of the candle and say the following (or similar) words:
  " I verify my capability to interact with stability."

- Place the final stone to the left of the candle, directly in line with the 3rd, and say the following words (or similar):
  " I stand in my sovereignty no matter the actions of others."
  Allow the candle to melt.

- Gather the stones into the bag and keep it with you throughout the upcoming encounter.

- Visualize the stones creating a protective shield around you as you browse the conversation(s).

Scrying With The Use of Tiger's Eye

Tiger's eye has to do with both the Sun and the Earth, which makes perfect sense considering its interwoven layers of brown and gold. This stone is also a promoter of energetic interaction between the physical and spiritual realms.

This spiritual technique uses the shinning exterior of polished tiger's eye stones, in addition to water and sunlight, to assist in striking visual images that can communicate messages to the receptive practitioner. It is best carried out outside on a sunny day, but if this isn't possible, a warm or sunny window can also work.

You will need:

- Many (about 10 to 20) small to medium tiger's eye stones
- Writing paper or Journal
- Glass dish
- Sunshine
- Cup of water

Directions:

- Place the tiger's eye stones in the glass dish.

- Put the water over the stones until the dish is almost full (but don't let it spill over the edge).

- Have some deep breaths to clear your mind.

- Keeping your focus mild, gaze on the small pool of water and the reflections of the stones. Be open to any images or visions that develop.

- Try to record your images and ideas in your journal to explore further when you have finished.

CHAPTER SIXTEEN

Jet

Unlike the other crystals and stones included in this collection, the jet is a fossilized wood rather than a real gem. As the araucaria trees of the Jurassic duration began to die off, their rotting wood ended up in swamps, rivers, and other bodies of water. The wood was eventually flattened by the pressure of multiple layers of organisms and mud over millions of years. When grand tree into gleaming black stones, Chemical alters eventually morphed the residues of this.

Named from a region in Asia Minor, the color of this stone is the source of the phrase "jet black," used to describe anything as black as it is possible to be. Some specimens might, in fact, be browner in color.

Jet has been used because prehistoric times-- it has been found in burial mounds as far back as 1400 BCE-- and was treasured for its protective residential or commercial properties by ancient travelers and soldiers alike. It is a soft, dull stone in rare type; the jet can endure a high amount of polishing, which enables it to take on a mirror finish. It was frequently used for this function during medieval times.

It was also widely known in many cultures during this duration that breathing in the smoke from the burning jet was physically and spiritually useful. In more recent history, plane became well-known as a "mourning stone" after Queen Victoria of England used it while mourning the death of her other half, Prince Albert.

Like lots of black stones, jet gets rid of undesirable energetic attachments and soaks up negativeness. It's an excellent stone for meditation and recovery sorrow. Related to the planet Saturn and the Element of Earth, a jet is used in magical workings connected to filtration, psychic security and increased psychic awareness, promoting luck associated with money, and prophecy. Like malachite, it is known to increase the efficiency of magic when put on the altar or other work areas.

The spells listed below show you how to use the jet to develop a pendant to ward off headaches, to clean your aura, to support yourself during a time of sorrow, and to promote success at a brand-new job.

Anti-Nightmare Protection Charm

Jet is a terrific stone to use in sleep magic, specifically for those who experience nightmares or other sleep disturbances. Jet beads can be discovered through crystal and mineral retailers and at craft shops(though make sure to check at craft shops that you're not getting replica glass beads). If nothing else, you can buy a jet locket or bracelet and unstring it to create this sleeping beauty from scratch.

You will need:

- 10 to 15 jet beads
- A number of inches of thick silver thread
- Scissors
- Thumb-tack or hook
- Work candle for atmosphere (optional).

Guidelines:

- Light the candle.
- Spend a long time taking deep breaths and quieting your mind. Start by cutting a long piece of silver thread when you're ready.
- Connect a knot at the end of the thread, making it big enough that the jet bead will not slip off.
- Place one bead on the thread and state the following (or similar) words:

" Peaceful sleep I shall find, all my headaches, I now bind.".

- Connect a knot and then repeat the chant as you put the next bead on the thread. Repeat this process until all the beads have been strung.
- Use the scissors to cut the thread, leaving enough to tie a small loop. Use the loop to hang the pendant on a tack or hook above your bed.

Aura Purification Ritual.

Everyone has an aura, the subtle energy field that surrounds us and extends externally from our physical form. Our thoughts, actions, diet, and physical environment have an impact on our aura so that it changes depending on how we're thinking and feeling, and how we're treating our bodies and minds. Those who can see atmospheres can inform if an individual's overall energetic state is healthy or in requirement of assistance, based upon the vibrancy (or do not have thereof) of the colors swirling in their auric field.

You do not require to be able to see your aura, however, to know if you're energetical "down in the dumps." This spell uses the cleansing properties of a jet to clean dirty or stagnant energies in your auric field. Use it in conjunction with healthy food, workout, and regular meditation (or other spiritual activity) to keep your aura vibrant and lively.

You will need:

- Several (10 to 30) pieces of jet.
- Pillows.
- Small fabric bag (optional).
- Work candle for atmosphere (optional).

Guidelines:

- Light the candle, if using.
- Take three deep breaths and launch any little disruptions from your day on each exhalation.
- Lie down in a comfortable position on your flooring, using pillows to support yourself so that you can fully unwind.
- Place the jet stones around the boundary of your body, paying conscious attention to each positioning.
- Now take more deep breaths and start to cause your pineal eye, or" second sight.".
- Starting with your feet, psychologically scan each part of your body. As you move gradually up your body, be conscious of any part that feels stuck, dark, or otherwise less-than-optimal in terms of energy. Don't over examine this. Instead, let your intuition guide you.
- Imagine a white light over any location you feel is energetically deteriorated or out of balance, to send out power and energy back to that area.

- When you have finished a full scan of your body, feet, calves, knees, thighs, groin, intestines, stomach, chest, neck, arms, hands, and head, picture your entire body loaded with white light.
- Continue to lie there and relax completely for 10 to 15 minutes.
- You may wish to keep the jet stones in a small bag to use each time you need to clean your aura.
- Make sure to clean the stones in between uses, by smudging them with sage or smoke from a purification incense.

Routine for Easing Grief.

When someone you're close to hand down to the next world, it's essential to enable yourself to grieve. Grieving is a natural and healthy response to loss. But grief is a process, and eventually, it is necessary to let go of pain and progress with our lives. If you find that after much time has passed, you are not making development in this regard, a routine of memorial can help.

Jet's ability to assist with the purification of undesirable energies makes it an appropriate stone in this circumstance. Jet assists in increased psychic awareness, which can help you sense when your liked one is near, supplied you are open to it.

In this routine, you will be commemorating positive memories of your enjoyed ones. You will also be speaking of these memories aloud, as providing a voice to your experiences with this person will assist you launch sadness that has ceased to serve its purpose. If you are open to it, you might notice that your enjoyed one is listening, and adoringly appreciating your honoring of them in the physical world.

You will need:

- Several (10 to 20) jet beads.
- Pendant cord with clasp or thick thread.
- White candle.

Guidelines:

- Light the candle and take three deep breaths.
- Holding a jet bead in one hand and the locket cable or thread in the other, remember a pleasant memory of the person you are grieving. This can be a specific story, a character characteristic you admired in the person, or something joyful about your relationship with them.
- Speak out loud about this memory. If you feel likely, speak to the person.
- After speaking of the memory out loud, string the bead onto the cable or thread.
- Repeat this procedure for each of the jet beads.

- Protect the clasp or connect a knot in the thread when you have finished.
- You may wish to wear the beads as a pendant, place them on your altar, or hang them in a special place in your home.
- In the future, you might feel that it's time to let go of the string of beads or keep them in a place where you will not see them. This is fine, and ought to be taken as a sign that you have progressed substantially in your mourning procedure.

Jet Gifting Spell.

There are ethical concerns to be mindful of when it comes to working magic for others. Because everyone's course in life is genuinely their own, it's not up to us to cast spells for others without their approval, no matter how benevolent our objectives are. If you are asked to work a period for somebody else, then, by all means, do so. What if you want to provide a wonderful present to somebody who wouldn't think or understand in magic?

This spell is an excellent example of how you can share your beautiful talents with others without being unknowingly manipulative or needing their permission. It can be done with any stone for any function, however here we will deal with a particular custom offering jet to a person who has just landed a brand-new job.

Jet is a powerful beacon of best of luck, helpful energies, and personal calmness as well as stability under pressure. It is thought about the ideal gemstone to provide to somebody unique to honor their beginning in a new task. This necessary act is an excellent method to use your positivity and impressive skills to commemorate a pal and honor's or others enjoyed one's accomplishment. You can tell them that jet is a traditional best of luck stone for those who are beginning new tasks. Whether or not you inform them that you charged it with your own positive energy is up to you.

You will require:.

- Jet stone or piece of precious jewelry featuring jet.
- Small jewelry box.

Directions:.

- Place the jet stone or piece of fashion jewelry on the altar or table in front of you. Take a few minutes to concentrate on the recipient, noting the positive aspects of their character and the skills they will bring to their brand-new position. Picture them in their brand-new task achieving success and content.

- Concentrate your positive vibrations into the things by putting your hands above the jet.
- Place it in a little box when you have thoroughly imbued the stone with your positive and motivating energy.
- Offer the present to your friend or liked one and understand that each time they wear the precious jewelry or location the stone in a space at their new position, they will be filled with the good desires you have meant for them.

CHAPTER SEVENTEEN

Hematite

One of the common minerals on Earth is hematite, it was discovered in nations as far apart as Brazil, Norway, Italy, and Canada. In its pure type, hematite can typically develop into structures that appear to have petals like a flower.

The name hematite originates from the Greek word haimatites, which roughly equates to "blood," due to its ochre interior. In truth, for numerous centuries, hematite was called "bloodstone," though we now use that name for the green jasper featured previously in this book. A minimum of one misconception about the stone'sorigins was associated with the fight. As soldiers lay hurt in the consequences of a match, big pools of blood would collect and sink into the earth, forming the mineral.

Hematite's smooth, glasslike surface made it an ideal crystal for use as a primary mirror in ancient times. The powdered interior was used as a pigment in some cavern paintings, and by the ancient Egyptians who painted their pharaoh's tombs and sarcophaguses to illustrate pictures of the afterlife. Native Americans also used hematite to paint their faces before going into battle.

Despite its lots of associations with blood and battle, hematite is likewise understood as a stone linked to the higher mind. It helps to center and organize energy by grounding and relaxing the user. The ability to focus while experiencing numerous stimuli simultaneously can help to lower stress and anxiety in social situations. Associated with Mars and Saturn, and the Elements of Fire, Earth, and Water, hematite is used in beautiful functions related to grounding, psychic awareness, recovery, past-life recall, crucial and rational thinking, self- esteem and confidence, and dissipating unfavorable energy in one's environments.

The spells in this chapter use hematite to assist you in releasing concern endanger, transform pessimism into optimism, and ground yourself during social interactions that may trigger increased stress and anxiety.

Spell to Boost Optimism.

Anyone who comprehends the Law of Attraction understands that our ideas develop our reality. Hematite's grounding and healing homes can be used to help you turn your mindset around and go back to drawing in positive thoughts and experiences.

The hematite in this spell works on two levels. It helps you in reprogramming your unfavorable ideas into favorable declarations. It likewise wards off any other general unfavorable energy that you might have been unwittingly bringing in during your bout with cynical thinking.

You might be able to recognize a wide variety of unfavorable thoughts; it's best to just work with a small handful, to focus your objective on the act of transmuting the hostile into positive. Otherwise, you may get overwhelmed, or your focus might dissipate through the effort of rewriting a lot of separate ideas. Simply focus on the primary concerns that have been coming up for you repeatedly.

You will need:

- 3 to 5 hematite stones.
- 3 to 5 little slips of paper.
- White candle.

Directions:

- Light the candle and invest a long time quieting your mind.
- When you're all set to begin, recall a particular negative thought that you have been having recently.
- Among the slips of paper, rewrite the negative thought into a favorable statement. If you keep thinking, "I never

have any money," you can write, "I believe cash can stream to me without having to know its source.".

- Wrap the slip of paper around the hematite stone so that the words are dealing with the outside.
- Protect the paper with a drop of wax.
- Repeat this process with the remaining hematite and paper.
- Leave the paper-wrapped stones on your altar or place them in an area where you spend a lot of time, to assist you keep in mind to transform your negative thoughts into positive declarations.
- When you are downhearted, "funk" has raised, thank the stones and recycle the slips of paper.

Spell to Ease Social Anxiety.

Those who struggle with social stress and anxiety understand that it doesn't just occur in significant group circumstances. Depending on your level of sensitivity to other individuals' energy, anxiety can crop up throughout all sorts of encounters with other individuals.

In this spell, you will create a useful talisman to carry in your pocket, assisting you to keep in mind to ground and center yourself throughout social interactions.

You will require:

- One medium hematite stone.
- White or black spell candle.

Instructions:

- Light the candle and invest some time breathing deeply to peace your mind. When you feel ready, spend a few minutes imagining the sort of social situation that makes you uneasy.
- Ask yourself what activates an anxiety-producing reaction in your body during these scenarios.
- When you identify a trigger, get the hematite and hold it in between your palms.
- Take a deep breath in and out slowly, counting to 7.
- Imagine yourself in this imagined social setting, surrounded by white light. Repeat this breathing procedure three times, focusing on filling the stone with tranquil, relaxed energy.
- Now, place the hematite in front of the candle.
- Enable it to charge there till the candle has burned all the method down.

- Bring the charmed stone with you in your bag or pocket the next time you are participating in a social scenario that might produce a nervous reaction. You can hold on to the stone throughout any hard minutes without anyone even understanding!

Anger Release Spell.

Anger is a normal human feeling that fits, briefly, in specific scenarios. It's best for your health-- psychological, spiritual, and physical launch anger once it has served its purpose. This spell will assist you to remove the energy of sticking around bitterness and move on so that you can experience positive emotions, like hope, love, and joy, more completely and clearly.

Hematite's recovery homes and its ability to dissipate negativeness makes it an excellent stone for this sort of work. The Earth's power to transmute negative energy into positive or neutral energy is also made use of in this spell. Raw hematite is best for burying, but a sleek stone will likewise operate in a pinch.

You will need:

- Small to medium raw hematite stone.
- Black or white candle.

- Journal or writing paper (optional).

Instructions:.

- Light the candle, and invest some time quieting your mind.
- Allow yourself to focus on the anger and bitterness you're still carrying with you from an old scenario.
- If it assists, do some freewriting about the issue, try to determine the factors for the anger you're still feeling.
- Hold the hematite in between your palms when you're all set.
- Imagine the feelings you're wanting to release streaming into the stone, making it grow warm and more oppressive in your hands.
- Go outdoors and bury the stone in the Earth.
- As you dig the little hole and cover the stone, say the following (or similar)words:

" Let this bottled-up anger stop. These old sensations I now release. I blessed Be.".

Spell to Release the Habit of Worry.

Preparation ahead is a valuable skill to have in life, but continuously stressing about what might or may not occur is really detrimental to manifesting the truth you want. If you're a chronic worrier, you're certainly not alone.

However, you can empower yourself to ditch this practice with the help of the powers of Nature. The soothing effect of running water in this spell combines with the transmuting power of hematite to help you launch your routine of stressing and clear up your energy field for a smoother, more carefree life. You can put the stones in a bowl and run water from the sink or bathtub over them for many minutes and if you do not live near a stream or creek.

Spread the stones over the Earth. It's hugely recommended that you make an effort to bring them to a natural body of water, even if you have to go out of your method to get there.

You will require:

- Some raw hematite stones.
- Little cloth bag.

Instructions:.

- Spend some time quieting your mind.
- Take one stone and hold it between your palms when you feel prepared. Consider a specific concern that you are currently experiencing and let the hematite absorb the fears. Place it in the little bag.

- Continue this procedure with as many stones as you require. Bring the bag of hematite to a nearby stream, river, or creek.
- Sit silently for a couple of minutes at the edge and enable the sound and sight of the moving water to relieve your spirit.
- When you feel ready, carefully empty the bag of stones into the running water. Thank the Elemental spirits of the water for cleansing your energy of concern and fear.
- The next time you find yourself starting to anticipate something unfavorable happening in the future, return in your mind to the water running over the hematite stones.
- If you can, enter the practice of listening to recordings of a bubbling brook, a waterfall, or perhaps the ocean to assist you preserve a calmer mindset.

CONCLUSION

This marks the completion of the WiccaBook. You are now geared up with the necessary fundamentals and the knowledge to make your very first actions in the Craft and in understanding the fundamentals of the religion of Nature that is Wicca. The most excellent thing you can do for yourself is to acquire as much knowledge as possible on the Craft and Wiccan religion to train yourself in practice and to forge your journey with enjoyment and fulfillment.

Throughout your journey and through every step of the way, continuously remember the Wiccan Rede, "AN' IT HARM NONE, DO WHAT THOU WILT."

CPSIA information can be obtained
at www.ICGtesting.com
Printed in the USA
BVHW042313271020
591817BV00029B/145

9 781801 12058